CONTENTS

CHAPTER I
PIGEONS IN HISTORY

The domestication of pigeons predates written history. People raised pigeons for food long before they were able to write. We cannot say for sure whether people adopted pigeons or if people were adopted by pigeons.

A pigeon has many natural enemies and no defense against them except in flight. Naturally, a pigeon will nest in the safest possible place. Where better than close to people, whose very presence would frighten away the pigeon's predators?

Today, common wild pigeons find shelter in our barns and buildings. In larger cities, they nest comfortably in man-made structures like the lofts of buildings, on ledges, roofs and crannies, under bridges and in elevated structures. It seems likely that the early pigeon nested near people, perhaps in the same caves, or in the roofs of their dwellings.

Tender young squabs almost ready to leave the nest would have been a tasty morsel then, as they are today. So the story of early pigeon raising might be summed up in a few sentences. People built houses. Wild pigeons liked the protection of those houses and moved close to them. People liked to eat young squabs, and that was the beginning of pigeon husbandry.

The Old Testament of the Bible describes the use of pigeons as sacrifices to God around the year 1900 B.C. Near the time of Christ, the ancient Romans bred pigeons, and their written records describe several different breeds.

In ancient Greece, the Olympic Games were as popular as World Series baseball is in our country today. Whole towns would anxiously await news, especially if a favorite son was a contender in one of the events. In that era, pigeons were the messengers, and would quickly carry news of the winner back to their home towns.

The ruler of Baghdad established a regular news service, pigeon powered, in the middle of the twelfth century. There are accounts of pigeon races held in Belgium as early as 1700. The early settlers of the United States and Canada brought their pigeons with them. A letter dated 1621, written by the Governor of Virginia to the Governor of Massachusetts, listed, among other items, that pigeons ". . . were being forwarded." An early drawing of the city of Quebec, dated 1608, pictures a "pigeon habitation." Other writers tell of pigeons being raised in Nova Scotia by the French in 1605.

There were nearly 200 Belgian immigrants who lived in Midwestern towns by the Mississippi River and who flew Racing Homers. These birds are descendants of stock brought with these Belgium families. They kept their strains pure.

Yellow Reverse-wing Pouter. Bred by L. & B. Beer, Lindenhurst, New Jersey.

Many an American veteran owes his life to the faithful performance of the Homing pigeon. In World War I the army pigeon, *Cher Ami,* flew 25 miles in 25 minutes. Even with his leg shattered by shrapnel and a ragged hole in his breast, he delivered word of the plight of the "Lost Battalion." In October, 1943, G.I. Joe flew 20 miles in 20 minutes and saved the lives of 1,000 Allied soldiers. The message he carried prevented Allied artillery from shelling ground captured ahead of schedule. Radio communications had failed and G.I. Joe arrived just as bomber planes were set to take off.

On the Eastern front, Airborne Patrol dropped four-month-old Jungle Joe behind Japanese lines. He delivered a secret message which helped open a large part of Burma to Allied troops. Five-month-old Burma Queen, dropped by parachute to a unit surrounded by Japanese, flew 320 miles over rugged mountain country to save the lives of the hard-pressed troops.

CHAPTER 2
BREEDS AND VARIETIES

Ornithologists have classified more than 500 species of wild pigeons and doves. They believe our own domestic pigeons descended from the wild Rock Pigeon, subfamilies of which are found today in Asia, Africa, and Europe. Others theorize that not one, but several species of wild doves may have been the ancestors of our present domestic pigeons.

Regardless of ancestry, more than 175 breeds of pigeons are listed in pigeon books today. The exact number is unknown. Some of the older breeds have disappeared and new breeds are being developed each year.

Breeders have developed an astounding number of varieties and subdivisions of variety by color in many of the 175 or more breeds. For instance, Modenas are bred in 152 varieties. In Fantails, you find White and six standard colors. Those six colors may also develop into different patterns, like Saddles, Tailmarks, and Bodymarks. Thus we quickly count twenty-five varieties in Fantails alone, and there are still others.

Both the Pouter family and its closely related Cropper family are huge. The Oriental group alone would fill a book. A slight change in color pattern, or perhaps the presence of a crest or of feathered feet may mark the only difference between two breeds.

This book was not intended to be a fanciers' standard. A few breeds of pigeons the average person might encounter will be briefly described on the following pages.

FLYING BREEDS

Racing Homers

Solid, tight-feathered and exceptionally rugged individuals. Mature males weigh 14 to 16 ounces, females 11 to 13 ounces.

Most of today's strains can be traced back to Belgian fanciers of 200 to 300 years ago.

This breed exemplifies "the survival of the fittest." Poor or weak birds didn't find their way back home from the races. Only the strong survived, and these were used as breeders. As a result the Racing Homer is a tough, self-reliant individual, able to take care of itself under all conditions.

Young Racing Homers are often flown up to 300 miles in their first year. Old, well trained birds will return home from distances of 500 to 1000 miles.

Racing Homer squabs weigh eight to ten pounds per dozen. Homer squabs are often raised for home use where size of squab is not a monetary factor.

"Patricia"
Combine Winner
MN State Race

Clair Hetland
Golden Valley, MN

AU.92 MPLS.2210

foto: Henk Kuijlaars

Racing Homer loft in Spring Hill, Florida.

Because they seldom break eggs or trample squabs, Homers are often used as feeders (foster parents) for hard-to-raise breeds, such as those pigeons with short beaks.

Old birds purchased from another loft for breeders should be kept confined as "prisoners," or they might attempt the journey to their original home. Only the young birds raised in your own loft should be allowed to fly free.

Ceremonial White Pigeons

Recent years have witnessed the rise of a cottage industry which could be perfect for certain fanciers. What could make an event more delightful for its audience than the dramatic release of beautiful white homing pigeons? This can be a nice source of extra income if it is done correctly. As a pigeon fancier, one already has most of the necessities in place.

Many people are looking for white pigeons, or "white doves," for such releases. They can't find you, so you must find them. Print up some business cards and leave them with funeral directors, set up a booth at bridal fairs, contact retail stores about grand openings, and so on. Network and use your imagination to reach all potential markets.

Entrepreneurs should set up for this little business with style. Some recommendations: find a nice wicker crate, paint it white and keep it scrupulously clean. Always arrive dressed neatly, and be prepared to wear whatever type of outfit that anyone, especially the bride, would request.

It is important to think through the details of your release. For example, you should transport the birds in a pickup or van, never in the trunk of a car. Why? Rumor tells of a young man who had successfully booked weddings for an entire summer. He had a big wedding for the local banker lined up for a $300 release. He boxed the birds in cardboard boxes and put them in the trunk of his car. When time came for the release all the birds had suffocated. What a send off for a marriage!

Funerals are very touching places for white pigeon releases. For a Christian burial you could supply three birds. The minister gently releases the birds one by one, saying "In the name of the Father, the Son, and the Holy Ghost." There are no dry eyes.

What a disappointment the 1996 Olympics in Atlanta became without the traditional and spectacular release of a huge flock of pigeons at the Opening Ceremonies!

Finally, if you are not interested in releasing pigeons, consider raising quality white pigeons to sell. Finding white pigeons that are dependable and will come home under all conditions is not easy. If you have the right stuff you will have a nation-wide market.

Birmingham Rollers

The Birmingham Roller, believed to have originated within the Tumbler family, has for all practical purposes evolved into two separate breeds: the Show Roller and the Flying, or Competition Roller.

As the names imply, the Show Roller is bred primarily for the show cage and the flying roller is bred primarily for performance. Since the late 1970s, the Show Roller has increased in size and

Classic Black Baldhead Birmingham Roller.
Bred by Richard Nauer, Osseo, Minnesota.

feather until it now bears little resemblance to the more trim and dapper Flying Roller. Great emphasis is placed on the head and neck style and the bird's "station," or how they position themselves in the show cage, when selecting the best Show Roller.

The performance standard for the Flying Roller calls for the bird to spin backward somersaults while falling through the air. The faster the somersaults, called velocity, the better the performance. Rollers are also valued according to their frequency, or how many times they perform in a twenty minute flying period, and their depth, or how deep they fall when spinning their somersaults. As one might guess, some roller fanciers value frequency, or depth, or velocity over the other two characteristics, thus leading to many different families of Rollers.

Rollers are usually flown in "kits," groups of twenty or so birds. The more birds "breaking" or performing together, the more valuable the kit. A 3/4 turn by fifteen or more birds breaking together is a sight to behold.

Flying competitions between Roller fanciers have grown greatly in popularity and size during the 1990s. The World Cup Competition, involving hundreds of competitors across the United States, Canada, England and a few countries in Europe, has done much to standardize judging for flying competitions and to popularize the breed.

A half-dozen or so national conventions for flying enthusiasts are usually held each year in the United States, attracting hundreds of fanciers. The conventions offer a chance to exchange ideas and breeding stock and observe local kits. Someone contemplating joining the roller fraternity should try to attend a convention as early on as possible.

The wonderful thing about Flying Rollers is that they can be enjoyed as a backyard hobby, a club level hobby, or an international hobby. Most Roller fanciers take advantage of all three.

Rollers themselves are an easy breed to raise. They are small in size, easy keepers, very prolific, and come in every color imaginable. Flying enthusiasts tend to favor multi-colored birds splashed with white in order to distinguish them while in the air.

Because of their small size and the fact they can be flown regularly, Rollers can be housed with a minimum investment. A kit of twenty birds can be housed quite satisfactorily in a pen 3' x 3' x 3'. A breeding pen 4' x 8' can easily house six breeding pairs, all that is needed to maintain two kits with plenty of birds.

Rollers should be considered by anyone contemplating raising pigeons for the first time, by seasoned pigeon fanciers desiring an enjoyable backyard hobby, and by those pigeon fanciers who enjoy competitions. They are truly a bird for all seasons.

At left, a Utility King for squab production.
Center, a Utility Giant Homer.
Right, a White Swiss Mondain.

UTILITY BREEDS

There are many types and strains of pigeons that qualify as utility breeds. Originally there were white, blue, and silver Kings as well as French Gros Mondains, White Swiss Mondains, Giant Homers, Carneau, and Hungarians. Most of these breeds have become show birds and are no longer good squabbers. The birds that work best as squabbers are the birds that raise nice plump squabs. Of course, there are some people who keep a flock of utility birds true to the old standard like the White Swiss Mondain. Using French Mondains for squabs is popular in the South.

Red Carneau

This breed was brought to America from France. Many soldiers of World War I remember it as the red pigeon of France that flew

A fly-pen (note the wire bottom) containing Utility King pigeons. Bred for squab production by Harold Wong, Bloomington, Minnesota.

wild there, foraging in the fields for its living. The first Carneau raised in this country were about the size of Racing Homers, their red plumage was liberally sprinkled with white. Their squabs were plump and light skinned, and the breed quickly replaced Homer breeders in many lofts. First known as *Carneaux*, American breeders have now shortened this to *Carneau*.

Selective breeding for size has resulted in a much larger Carneau today. This advantage has been offset by unwise breeding for deep red plumage which has almost spoiled the breed for commercial use.

White Carneau

American breeders are responsible for the creation of the White Carneau. Many of the original Red Carneau carried a lot of white in their plumage. This breed was crossed with other white American breeds and resulted in the White Carneau of today.

Although a few White Carneau of the show type are being bred today, as a general rule the breed has retained its fine working qualities.

This breed has been a great favorite in some of the larger squab operations in the southeastern part of the United States.

Hungarians

There is some question about whether Hungarians should be classed as a show type or a working breed. It might be used as either.

Hungarians originated in central Europe. Adults are long legged, short backed and very plump breasted. They are of medium size.

The Hungarian is one of the most strikingly marked of all breeds. Its two-color plumage may be Red, Yellow, Black, Dun, Blue or Silver, in each instance the contrasting color is white.

Very few Hungarians are found in commercial lofts. Those found in the United States are usually in the hands of breeders who keep them for showing or for their own pleasure.

This breed is a good one for squab raising. You could eat those that were badly marked and save the perfect specimens for stock.

Hungarians from an old print.

SHOW TYPE BREEDS

To explain the show type counterpart of utility pigeons one must go back to the beginning of the breeds. The White King provides a good example.

The first White Kings were utility type pigeons. As such they quickly replaced Homers and Carneau in commercial lofts. Their popularity grew as people wanted to see this new breed. Soon the White King found its way into the pigeon shows where it was exhibited with other pigeons of that day.

Most showmen are not content with second place. If their Kings do not win they hike for home and try to breed a bigger and

*Champion White Show King. Bred by
John A. Schroeder, El Cajon, California.*

better King to win another year. That is what happened, and here we had the beginning of breeding for show. Within ten to fifteen years two kinds or types of White Kings were being raised, one for raising squabs, one for show.

The utility type of King stayed as it had been in the beginning. It was a pigeon of medium size, streamlined, carried a tail of medium length in a horizontal plane or at a slight angle downward. Its purpose was to raise large squabs rapidly and efficiently and in this it excelled.

Using the Utility King as a start the show type breeder began making changes. He broadened the back, made the breast much

*Top left, Champion Giant Homer Cock.
Bred by M. Durkee, Winnebago, Minnesota.
Top right, White Carneau Cock. Bred by
Mel Sorensen, St. Francis, Minnesota.
Bottom left, Red Carneau Cock. Bred by
Mel Sorensen, St. Francis, Minnesota.
Bottom right, Giant Homer Hen.
Bred by M. Durkee, Winnebago, Minnesota.*

At left, a French Mondain cock. At right, a French Mondain hen. Both bred by Frank Wolfbauer, Anoka, Minnesota.

wider and deeper. He shortened the tail and pointed it upward. He beefed up the bird, adding a half pound or more weight on a heavier boned frame.

In swift succession we were to see Utility Silver Kings, then Show Type Silver Kings. We now have both Utility and Show Type French Mondains, which have the same blocky build as other show type breeds. The old Utility Type Carneau is almost never seen. It has passed out of the picture, but the show Carneau is with us in all colors.

In general the show type pigeon is larger, blockier and heavier than the utility pigeon of the same breed. The show type pigeons have been bred for exhibition. In bringing them to their present state of perfection they have lost some of their original abilities: careful feeding of young and rapid reproduction. In most instances the utility birds are the better squabbers of the two.

Buy the show type if your hobby is large and beautiful pigeons and rate of production is not of importance to you. Buy utility birds if you are in pigeons for the money that is to be made in raising squabs or future breeders.

ORNAMENTAL BREEDS

In this group we class the toy breeds, breeds with unusual body conformation, striking plumage pattern or arrangement of feathers, or some larger breeds most often seen in the show room. A few of these are briefly described in the following pages.

Fantails

Fantails were mentioned by some of the earliest writers. They were described as a broad tailed pigeon with a shaking motion, native to India. American, English, and Scottish breeders worked the breed over and brought it to its present standard.

Fantails should be kept confined to the loft and fly-pen. They are not strong flyers, can not see the approach of enemies from behind or ahead, and are easily caught by cats or dogs. Most strains raise their own young without trouble, make fine pets, are enjoyed by all who love fine pigeons.

The most popular colors are pure White, Black, Blue, Red, Yellow, Silver, Dun and Splashes. The colors not so commonly found are Saddles, Tailmarked (white bodied with colored tail) and Bodymarked (colored body with white tail).

Top, A champion White Fantail. Bred by Bob & Vida Given, St. Louis Park, Minnesota. **Bottom left** and **right,** Indian Fantails. Bred by Ron Ewing, Kansas City, Kansas.

Top left, a Pomeranian Pouter.
Top right, a Norwich
Cropper. At left, a
Pomeranian Pouter. All
bred by L. & B. Beer,
Lindenhurst, New Jersey.

Pouters

The Pouter family is large. From English breeders we have the English Pouter, Pigmy Pouter and Norwich Cropper. From Central Europe we have twenty-seven or more distinct breeds of Pouters and Croppers.

The large English Pouter and its smaller counterpart, the Pigmy Pouter, are most popular in America. Recently, many of the numerous breeds of Pouters from Central Europe are being exhibited in our larger pigeon shows.

Pouters of all kinds have always been a favorite of the fancy pigeon breeder. Good specimens are not easy to breed and are a challenge to even the most skilled fancier.

Tumblers

The Tumbler, one of the oldest breeds, is thought to have its origin in India or some other eastern country. Tumbling pigeons were described in English books as early as 1650 to 1700.

The first Tumblers were flying birds and performers. However, constant breeding to enhance show qualities has resulted in a Tumbler which today neither flies well nor is able to perform. Only the name remains.

As a show bird, the Tumbler is all that anyone could ask. It is bred in all colors, short faced and long faced, Muffed and Clean Legged. Some well-known color patterns are Almonds, Baldheads, Beards, Whitesides, and Badges.

Countries of central Europe have developed their own varieties of Tumblers. These European Tumbler breeds are seldom seen in the United States.

Rollers, Flights and Tipplers are all thought to have originated from Tumbler stock. They might be called the performing cousins of the Tumbler family.

Giant Runts

Ancient writings dating back to Biblical times describe a large pigeon, similar to a Runt, being raised for food in countries of southern Europe. Thus, the Runt is not only the largest, but one of the oldest breeds of domestic pigeons.

Because of its size and slow breeding qualities, it is not used commercially. Some of the most successful breeders confine each pair to a separate loft and fly-pen.

Many of the larger utility breeds of present day pigeons owe their size to liberal infusions of Runt blood. Early breeders crossed Runts with the smaller types of pigeons. Many of our present day large utility breeds have descended from such crosses.

Three photos of Giant Runts bred by John Delahoussaye, Cleveland, Mississippi.

Jacobins

"One of the fanciest of all fancy pigeons . . ." writes one pigeon author in describing the Jacobin. It is a small breed. A ruffle of feathers down the side of the neck (mane and rose) and a hood of feathers on top of the head shut off vision in all directions except forward.

Feathers of the hood should be trimmed back in breeding pairs to enable the pigeon to see in all directions. Colors are Black, White, Red, Yellow, Blue Bar and Silver. Primary wing feathers are usually white. The Jacobin is not a pigeon for the beginner. Only the most experienced should test his or her skill on a breed like this.

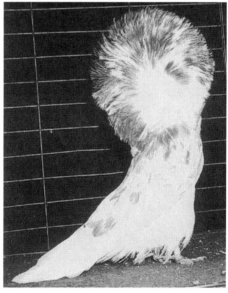

Champion Jacobins.
Bred by Ed Bachmann,
Pontiac, Michigan.

Modenas

All who love pigeons will enjoy the company of this charming and chesty little mite. Short coupled and chesty, round as a ball, the Modena looks exactly like a show type King in miniature.

Top left, Gazzi Modena. **Top right,** Blue Gazzi Modena. Both bred by Jim Abel, Kasson, Minnesota. **Bottom left**, Red Schietti Modena. **Bottom right,** Yellow Schietti Modena. Both bred by Ed Loomis, Lincoln, Nebraska.

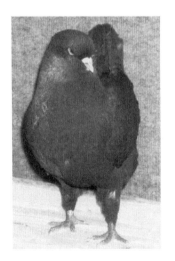

Body size is about the same as a Tumbler. Ambitious, raising their young easily, each pair turns out a surprising number of squabs in a season. Being extremely hardy and adaptable, the Modena is especially suited to younger people or those just starting with pigeons.

The Modena is bred in 152 or more color combinations. Those of one color are called Schietti, while those of two colors are Gazzi. In addition, there are many other varieties and sub-varieties based on coloring that make up this huge family.

*Bokhara Trumpeter, **left,** bred by Clair Hetland, Golden Valley, Minnesota. English Trumpeter, **right,** bred by Scott and Mira Perrizo, Lyons, Colorado.*

Trumpeters

Bokhara, English, and German are often seen at shows. The English is by far the most popular. The Bokhara is more difficult to raise, so it lacks the popularity of the English. The German is somewhere between the two breeds. Other strains are the Bernburg, Dresden, (both of which have beautiful coloring) and also the Altenburg. All of the various strains of Trumpeters maintain the "roll of the drum" voice characteristic.

CHAPTER 3

HOUSING

It is remarkable how little shelter pigeons need to survive. Common pigeons flying at large in our cities multiply so fast they are considered a nuisance. Their nests are built on cornices, under eaves, in cupolas, under railway bridges. Given a sheltered flat spot they construct their nest and rear their young.

The beginner planning a house for his or her flock should consider just what a pigeon needs. Listed in the order of their importance they are:

SHELTER. First of all, a pigeon needs a roof over its head. It must be protected from rain, snow and the elements when raising young. The pigeons' home may be anything from a box to an elaborate house, but it must have a roof.

DRYNESS. The house must be kept dry. Pigeons are not bothered by cold, they do not mind heat, but they must be dry. Pigeons actually suffer when housed in a damp building or one in which the floor is damp and sloppy. Several diseases of pigeons are caused by or aggravated by dampness.

PROTECTION. The house must not only shelter the pigeon and keep it dry, it must afford protection, too. It should be strong enough to protect the pigeon against rats, cats, dogs, and other predators. It is the pigeon's home, he should feel both safe and comfortable in it.

*Top left, an individual box for one pair. For settling or breeding. Note wire pull-out bottom for easy cleaning. **Top right,** individual boxes. Courtesy Peter Mesher, Plymouth, MN. **Bottom left,** a wire cage in back of garage makes a fine home for one pair. **Bottom right,** individual pens for mating or breeding. Courtesy of L. & B. Beer, Lindenhurst, New Jersey.*

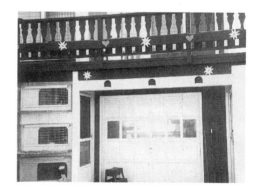

TYPES OF HOUSES

Loft for one to three pairs

Simple houses to accommodate one to three pairs can be made from large boxes. Old rabbit hutches can be used, each pair of pigeons being confined to a separate compartment. These small

*Small loft for Reverse-wing Pouters. Courtesy of
L. & B. Beer, Lindenhurst, New Jersey.*

boxes should be at least 30 inches square, 36 inches each way would be better. Height should be 24 to 30 inches. Back and sides should be enclosed, the front covered with wire. No fly-pen is needed.

A box three feet square and two feet high may be fastened to the inside wall of a barn or garage. This is living and nesting quarters. Cut a small opening through the side of the building as an entrance to the outside sun porch.

*Giant Homer loft of M. Durkee, Winnebago,
Minnesota. Note the wire bottom for birds in
fly-pen which helps to guarantee good health.*

The sun porch should be wire covered and as large or larger than the inside box. For two pairs, make the box larger and partition it. Both pairs could use a common sun porch.

Loft for five to ten pairs

If you expect to house as many as five to ten pairs of pigeons, you should provide them with better quarters, both for the well-being of the pigeons and for the convenience of the owner caring for them.

Any small room can be converted to a pigeon loft with little trouble or expense. A room 7 x 4, 8 x 12, or 10 x 10 feet will accommodate ten pairs or more of the largest breeds. An outside fly-pen or sun porch should be provided. Many pigeon lofts are simply an extra room in a barn or garage that has been converted. A small brooder house like those used to raise chicks makes an ideal pigeon loft.

Racing Pigeon loft of Clair Hetland—a converted garage.

Loft for twenty pairs or more

Never exceed 25 to 30 pairs of pigeons per pen. When more pairs are kept, the housing should be on a unit basis. Divide the birds into pens, each pen a separate unit with a fly-pen. 25 to 30 pairs per pen are recommended.

For reasons explained later in this book, each unit should be identical in size, equipment, and especially in the construction and location of the nests.

The best constructed lofts are 14 to 16 feet wide, the length being determined by the number of pens planned. The back four feet of the house is used as an alleyway, the front 10 to 12 feet as the pigeon pen proper. Each pen is 12 feet wide. The house may be 12, 24, 36, 48 feet, etc., long, depending on the number of pens desired. Each pen will house 25 to 30 pairs of breeders.

The front of the house may be open or closed, whatever is appropriate for the local climate. Floors may be wood, concrete or plain dirt. The area of the outside fly-pen should be the same as the inside room, 10 to 12 feet.

Racing Pigeon house, Spring Hill, Florida.

Details of pigeon loft construction:

ROOF. You may use any type of roof to build a pigeon house. The most preferable and cheapest to construct is the flat, shed type roof that slopes to the back. Any type of roof covering may be used.

FRONT. Climate determines the type of front to use. The open type front is best for those in the South, southeastern states, parts of California and areas where temperatures seldom fall below freezing. In other parts of the country the house must be closed on all sides.

FLOOR. Floors can be dirt, wood or concrete. A dirt floor will do if it is well drained and can be kept dry, but it can be difficult to keep out rodents. Wooden floors are very good because they are dry, tight, and easily cleaned. They should be far enough off the ground so rats and mice cannot work under them. Cement floors

End view of a simple pigeon house. This house is 10 feet wide,
8 feet at the front and 6 feet in the back. It may be built
10, 20, 30 or more feet long then divided into separate pens
each 10 feet square. Nesting units are mounted on inside
partitions. If the width of this house were increased to 13 feet, a
3 foot alleyway could be built inside the house at the rear.

*Top, a northern pigeon house. Faces south, alleyway runs full
length of back. Middle, a southern pigeon house. Note the
absence of front wall. Four foot overhang keeps out rain.
Courtesy of Palmetto Pigeon Plant, South Carolina.*
Bottom, *another northern house. This building has no alleyway,
doors open from pen to pen. Old Foy Pigeon Farm.*

are very good. Cover these with an inch or two of straw, cobs or litter.

FLY-PEN. There are two kinds of fly-pen: the elevated wire bottomed sun porch, or the regular fly-pen built from the ground up. The former has no perches. Flat perches or boards should be built around three sides of the latter.

The size of the outside fly-pen is governed by the amount of space you have available. It should not be smaller than the loft proper. If your loft is 10 x 10, your outside fly-pen should be at least that large. If you have plenty of room, a fly-pen 10 x 20 would be better. It should be as high as the eaves of your pigeon house.

When covering your fly-pen you should use either one or two inch mesh galvanized poultry netting. The two inch mesh wire will do the job. However, if you want to eliminate rats, sparrows and other small animals from your loft, it will pay you to use the smaller mesh netting.

The floor of the fly-pen may be of dirt, crushed rock or concrete. Some breeders prefer a floor of boards or wire raised 18 to 24 inches off the ground. A sun porch is easier to build, costs less, serves just as well as a fly-pen.

Location

The pigeon house should be located on a spot where the ground slopes away on all sides. This will provide good drainage away from the building. House and fly-pens should face the south whenever possible.

CHAPTER 4
EQUIPMENT FOR THE PIGEON HOUSE

Two kinds of equipment are needed for the pigeon house, that which is built in as a permanent part of the house, and that which is movable.

NESTS. These should be built as a part of the house. The three most important things to consider when building nests are: 1. There should be one double nest for each pair of pigeons in the pen. 2. The nest should be large enough for the breed. 3. Extra nests should be closed off when there are more nests than mated pairs in the house.

The only thing you need to build for the nest is a removable slide to fit the floor of each pigeonhole, which can be pulled out for cleaning. Construct this slide by cutting a board slightly smaller than the inside measurements of the bottom of the nest. Nail a two and one-half inch wooden strip across this false bottom. You can nail this strip across the front edge of the false bottom, but it is preferable to nail the strip about three to four inches back from the front edge. This makes the nest just a trifle smaller and is a help to the birds because they do not have to carry so much nesting material to make a suitable nest in this smaller nesting area. This strip also provides sort of a perch and lighting place for the birds in front of the nest.

Many a beginner has started with a loft of pigeons using orange crate nests, and even some of the large, successful, commercial pigeon plants still use them.

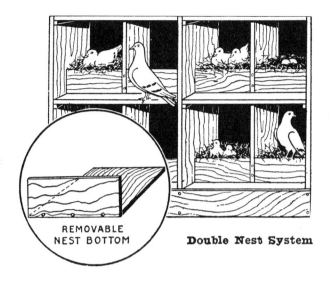

REMOVABLE
NEST BOTTOM

Double Nest System

*The nests have removable bottoms which rest on
cleats and can be easily removed for cleaning.*

Later, as your business grows, if you wish to build more attrac-
tive nests for your breeders, you might install the double nest system which is described next.

The Double Nest System

In this system nests are built in pairs with a six inch wide running
board in front of each double nest on which the parent birds may
pass from one nest to the other. Each double nest is divided from
the next door double nest by a full width partition. This enables
nesting birds to fight off any intruder that alights on the running
boards of their nests. At the same time, the wide partition prevents them from walking over to the neighboring nests and inter-
fering with the birds there.

The uprights should be of 3/4 to 1 inch lumber. The first
upright should be 18 inches wide, the second 12 inches, the third
18 inches, etc., alternating 12 and 18 inch uprights. Nail one inch

An ideal single nest arrangement for large pigeons.
Photo courtesy of Irvin T. Goss, Kentucky.

cleats 11 inches apart on both the 12 and 18 inch uprights to support the removable bottoms and the running boards. The running board is built of 3/4 to 1 inch lumber 23 inches long and 6 inches wide and is placed in front of the two nests between each 18 inch upright. The removable bottoms are built of 3/4 to 1 inch lumber 11 inches wide and 12 inches long. A three to four inch front piece is nailed across the end of each removable nest bottom. This will keep the nesting material, eggs, and young squabs from working out of the nest. Nest bowls are not needed with the double nest system but may be used if desired.

Provide one double nest for every pair of pigeons. It is a good plan to have only as many double nests as you have pairs. Should you have too many nests in your lofts, your birds will be tempted to move around and confusion results.

Perches are not necessary if you have a double nest for each pair of birds. You may, however, chose to outfit your loft with special perches, a variety of which are available from Foy's. The advantage of a tent type perch is obvious, birds don't foul the birds roosting below them. Clip on plastic tent type perches are popular because cleaning is as simple as popping the plastic and washing off the waste. The clip on system allows you to remove extra perches and prevent territory battles.

FEEDERS. Aisle feeders may be built into the partition between the back aisle of the house and the pen. It is convenient to feed from the outside of the pen, so birds are not disturbed. This system is best where pigeons are fed a mixture of grains or pellets twice daily.

Breeds like Runts, Mondains, Show Kings and Giant Homers require larger nests. Each compartment pictured on page 36 is 18 x 18 x 18 inches—large enough for force mating when using a nest front. Nests are 11 x 11 inches and slide out for cleaning. Two

AISLE FEEDING and WATERING SYSTEM
WATER
FEED TROUGH
AISLE

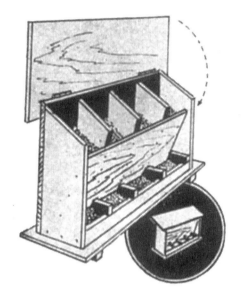

This cafeteria feeder, 30 inches long, 8 inches wide, 18 inches high at the back, is divided into four compartments. Feeding trough is 2 inches deep. Feed storage compartments are 8 inches wide at the top, 2 inches wide at the bottom. The opening through which feed moves from storage compartment to feeding trough is three-fourths inches high. Each compartment holds about 10 pounds of grain.

No-Waste Feeder. Pigeons can't throw feed out when looking for favorite seeds. These also work well for grit.

Wire guard and roost-proof cap protect this galvanized pan. May be used as a water pan, for feed, or for nesting materials.

week old squabs are placed under the nest and the old birds will lay again in the vacated nest.

At weaning time squabs find their way to the floor of the loft where they are occasionally fed by their parents. A hungry squab on the floor, begging for food, may get into trouble with pigeons that are not its parents, and it may be pecked to death or scalped.

Slatted container holds straw for nesting. Solid wooden top keeps straw clean.

Various two and a half gallon water fountains. Conetops can be added to galvanized metal fountains to prevent roosting.

Many squabs may be saved from injury or death if a 12 inch wide board is placed along one wall of the house about 5 inches off the floor. If a weanling squab on the floor then gets into serious trouble he will hurry under the shelter of the board where the older pigeons cannot peck him.

If you wish you may feed your pigeons cafeteria style. Use a feeder similar to the one pictured previously. Do not mix the feed. Keep each kind of grain in a separate compartment. A very good selection would be yellow corn, wheat, milo or kaffir, and peas in some form. Grit must be provided in a separate container.

The cafeteria feeder is used in many plants where large numbers of birds are housed and where labor costs are a factor. Using these, the chore of feeding is cut down to once a week. Pigeons balance their own ration and they seem to do just as well with this type of feeding as any other. Little or no feed is wasted when feeder is properly constructed.

It is important to the health of your birds that they do no eat dirty feed from the floor. The No-Waste Feeder carried by Foy's Pigeon Supplies addresses that problem. It has a trough design

Plastic feeders and waterers. Can also be used for grit. All available from Foy's.

with circles cut in plexiglass for individual feeding. Fanciers may have observed that birds toss essential protein-rich feeds such as peas and roasted soybeans right out of ordinary feeders. Grain will only be tossed around the interior of a No-Waste feeder.

A feeder that every bird can eat from at once is essential when birds are kept slightly hungry during training. Use either the galvanized 2 foot long feeder or the 2 foot wood dowel feeder. Four 2 foot feeders will feed sixty young homers at once. Birds will come in quickly when called, knowing tardiness means going hungry.

GRIT CONTAINERS are small but important. A small earthen crock is often used. Iron grit containers can rust out from the action of the salt on the metal. It is essential to keep grit clean, dry, and easy for birds to see and eat.

Some grit feeders do a good job of keeping grit clean and dry but birds cannot get at it easily. Try the cone top wire feeder or a medium size No-Waste feeder. Both allow birds easy access to grit. Several other grit feeders are shown in Foy's catalog.

NESTING MATERIAL is needed in every pen. A slatted box or a rack fastened to the wall and filled with straw or other nesting material should be provided. See picture.

WATERERS. Running water in the house is very handy especially if you tend many pigeons. By all means, use a good automatic fountain if you are in a part of the country where it seldom freezes. In the northern part of the U.S. automatic fountains are useful from May to October. When temperatures drop below freezing begin to use larger capacity metal fountains over heaters. Plastic water fountains may be used in rotation, when a fountain freezes up bring it in the house to melt. Do not try to break up ice by smashing the fountains or they will crack and leak.

Automatic waterers are best for squab operations and nice in the warmer states. While these waterers save time they still must be cleaned daily. They also have the disadvantage of being a poor way to deliver vitamins and medications to the birds.

There are many plastic fountains and hooded metal fountains that keep droppings out of the water. Foy's sells ten or twelve types. A good tip for keeping water clean is to place the water a couple of feet off the floor. This will help keep feathers and other material from the floor out of the water. You have to do all you can to keep water clean and prevent dirty drinking water—or "poop soup."

A mating coop is a handy piece of equipment in any pigeon house. It should be located out of sight of the other pigeons in the loft.

Pigeons to be mated are put in the coop, one on each side of the removable wire partition. After becoming acquainted by looking at each other through the wires for a few days, the partition is then removed. If they are old enough to mate and if they are male and female, the two will usually mate within a short time.

Leave them together in the coop for a few days until you are certain they are mated, then transfer them to the working pen. Read the section called "How To Settle New Pairs to the Loft" in Chapter 7.

BATH PAN. Any round pan four to six inches deep is satisfactory. A small dishpan makes a good one, as does a regular hog pan. It should be placed in the fly-pen. Use a good bath salt and leave the pan out for only an hour to prevent the birds from drinking the water. Pigeons enjoy bathing and should be provided with bath water several times a week.

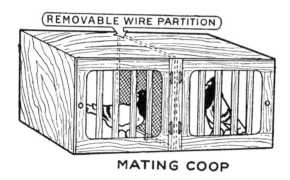

MATING COOP

CHAPTER 5
FEEDS AND FEEDING

A healthy pigeon needs three things to sustain life: feed, water and grit. All are equally important.

Wild pigeons live principally on grains and wild seeds found in the fields. Domestic pigeons are grain eaters and seldom eat worms, grubs or insects.

When buying grains for your pigeons there are three important facts to remember:

1. Never feed new grain right out of the field.
2. Never feed grain that is spoiled in any way.
3. Whenever possible, feed a mixture of grains.

New Grain

The average beginner with pigeons does not realize the importance of feeding old, seasoned grain. If at all possible, obtain grain harvested the previous season. The moisture content in old grain is low, usually old grain is dry, hard, sound and the pigeons thrive on it.

Recently harvested grain, right out of the fields, or less than three months old, simply does not agree with pigeons. If much new grain is fed you will soon find your old birds out of condition. Their feathers will ruffle, some will vomit, others will show signs of diarrhea.

The young squabs in the nest will be affected even quicker than the older pigeons. Many squabs in the nest may die within a few days after new, unseasoned grain is fed to the parent birds.

Spoiled Grain

A pigeon will stand heat, cold, neglect and abuse, but a few kernels of moldy grain will often kill it. Never feed corn that shows black spots of mould on the kernel. Grain will spoil in storage under two conditions, which you must look for and prevent. During the warm spring and summer months, shelled corn will heat in the bin and take on a bad odor. Corn or any other grain that has heated is not fit for pigeons. If a grain was too wet when shelled, it may begin to germinate and rot.

An easy way to detect mould or spoilage in the grain is to rub a small handful briskly between the palms of the hands, then smell it. Your nose will soon tell you if the grain is moldy or musty.

Care of Grain

The best grain will spoil if kept in a poor place. Wooden, mouse-proof bins are ideal storage places. Feed kept in sacks should never be set on a cement floor. The feed draws moisture from the cement floor; soon you have moldy feed. Always lay a few wooden boards on the floor, then pile the grain sacks on top of the boards.

Kinds of Grain to Feed

Pigeons do best if fed a variety of grains. For instance, they would exist for a long time on corn and peas alone, but they would do a whole lot better if their rations consisted of four grains instead of two.

There are some 15 to 20 kinds of grains and legume seeds suitable for pigeons commonly raised in the United States. Three or four of these grains are probably raised in your section of the country. Therefore, it is possible to mix an adequate grain ration for your pigeons using home grown grains, regardless of where you live.

Corn

Whole yellow corn is obtainable in all parts of the United States. It is one of the best of pigeon feeds. It may be used in quantities up to 50% of the entire ration. Yellow corn is high in Vitamin A. Feed up to 50% corn in winter and cool months. During hot summer months cut this down to 25% to 30%.

White corn may be fed in place of yellow corn. White corn is deficient in Vitamin A and should not be used unless yellow corn is unobtainable.

Cracked Corn

Some breeders feed cracked corn. Our experience is that cracking corn is extra work and a needless expense. Most breeds of pigeons, large or small, will swallow whole kernels of corn. Since cracked corn absorbs moisture and moulds quickly, it should be fed within a few days after cracking.

Wheat

Wheat is second in importance of the grains fed in the pigeon ration. Grown in almost all parts of the United States, it may be fed in amounts up to 35% of the entire ration. Although lacking in Vitamin A, it contains an abundance of the other vitamins needed to establish fertility and hatchability. The red varieties of wheat are superior to the white. Kaffir or milo may be used as a substitute if wheat is not available.

Kaffir or Milo

Although the two are separate grains, they are so closely related that they may be used interchangeably as a feed for pigeons. Either may be used in place of the other in any ration.

Both add variety to the grain mixture, both are relished by the pigeons in moderate amounts. 15% to 20% of the total grain ration may be kaffir or milo in the colder months. As much as 25% to 30% may be fed during the summer months, when part of the whole yellow corn may be replaced by these grains.

Oats

Whole oats should not be fed to pigeons. They contain a high percentage of fiber, apparently too much for the pigeon to handle. Hulled oats have been found to be a good pigeon feed, but they are too expensive to be practical.

Barley

A high fiber feed with good protein content is recommended for frequent use. It is a good feed that pigeons thrive on. Lazy pigeons that won't exercise will soon become active when fed 50% barley. Feed unmated hens 100% barley to keep them in shape and to prevent them from laying.

Rye

Rye may be fed to pigeons in small amounts. For some reason the pigeons do not seem to like it as well as other grains. It is not one of the staple grains for pigeons. If rye of good quality is easy to get and considerably cheaper than wheat, then rye may be substituted for wheat in the ration.

Rice

Polished rice may be fed in small amounts if cheap and convenient. Not more than five to ten pounds should be used per 100 pounds of total grain ration.

Buckwheat

Five to ten percent of buckwheat may be added to the grain ration. Pigeons seem to relish a small amount of this grain. Use only if convenient and cheap.

Legume Seeds

No mixture of pigeon grain is either complete or adequate unless it contains about 20% of peas of some kind. Peas complete the four basic ingredients. Corn, wheat, and kaffir are the other three.

Metal grit feeder keeps grit clean and dry. Has an added advantage over many others because pigeons can easily see the grit and will eat it much more readily. May also be used for grain or water.

Corn, wheat and kaffir contain approximately 9%, 11% and 13% of protein respectively. But a pigeon needs a total protein intake of about 15%. In order to raise the protein intake of the pigeon some HIGH PROTEIN legume must be added. Peas containing 23% to 25% protein will bring up the protein content of the entire ration if added in proper amounts.

Peas

The kind of peas you feed in your pigeon ration may depend on your location. In the northern part of the United States the field pea (sometimes called Canadian Pea) and the garden pea are easiest to obtain. Either may be used in the pigeon ration. In the southern or warmer states, one of the varieties of cow peas (southern field pea) or the black-eyed pea may be used. The kind of pea included in the ration is not important. Pigeons will eat one variety as well as the other once they become used to them.

Substitutes for Peas

In some parts of the country peas cannot be obtained, or if obtainable are so high in price they can not be used for pigeon feed. In such instances pelleted poultry feeds have been used as a substitute for peas.

The 3/16 inch size pellet is the best. You can use a layer pellet for hens, a starter, broiler, or turkey pellet for chicks. One kind of pellet seems to work as well as the other. The protein content should be between 20% and 25%. The amount of protein is always given on the analysis tag on the bag.

Some breeders feed all pellets, no grain. Others use half pellets, half grain and others 25% pellets, 75% grain. Old pigeons accustomed to grain often do not want to eat pellets. They will eat the grain first and leave the pellets. In these instances the birds have to be starved in to eating the pellets. This is usually harder on the owner of the pigeons than the on birds themselves. Once pigeons have learned to eat pellets they will consume them readily without further trouble.

When pigeons are fed all pellets, no grain, the droppings are often loose and very moist. This may present a cleaning problem in freezing weather because the droppings will accumulate in piles, freezing solid.

Experienced breeders add 50% corn to the winter pellet ration, feeding half corn, half pellets. Since corn is heat-producing, the pigeons relish the added grain in freezing weather. Furthermore, the addition of grain to the ration dries down the droppings to the point where they do not freeze.

A word of caution when using pellets, use only the non-medicated pellets—some pellets contain Arsenic to prevent coccidiosis. This treatment is intended for chicks and can be harmful to pigeons.

Soybeans

Although the soybean is a splendid feed for some animals, it should not be fed to pigeons in its natural state. Soybeans are high in protein and very high in fat. They may be fed to pigeons if first roasted in an oven at about 350 degrees for two to three hours. Roasting changes the indigestible proteins of the soybean to a form of protein the pigeon is able to digest. Pigeons relish fresh roasted soy beans. Beware—soybeans go rancid in 6 to 8 weeks and birds will not eat them. Only buy 100 pounds at a time.

Vetch

Vetch is grown in a few scattered sections of the United States. It may be used as a substitute for peas in the pigeon ration.

Peanuts

Shelled peanuts may be used as a substitute for peas. It is seldom practical to feed them because they are higher in price than other feeds. Pigeons love peanuts. You can tame the wildest pigeon if you can feed a few peanuts by hand. You must introduce the young bird's palate to the taste by cracking the peanuts into the feed a few times. Birds accustomed to the taste will follow you around the coop for more peanuts!

Peanuts can be used to put weight on a pigeon. Some breeds have standards which require a heavy show bird. Peanuts will successfully fill out a bird's frame.

Methods of Feeding

The small fancier with only a few pairs often prefers to feed his or her pigeons by hand, scattering the grain on the floor of the loft morning and evening. This is a good opportunity to observe the pigeons and get better acquainted with them. Hand fed birds soon become very tame, and are easily caught and handled by their owner.

All pigeon feeds are not perfectly balanced. If you feed by hand, take the time to watch which kinds of grain your pigeons eat first, and which grains they leave. Your pigeons will soon tell you if anything is wrong with the ration.

For instance, if they eat all the other grains and leave the corn, there is too much corn in the ration. If they eat the corn first and leave the other grains, they need extra corn. Correct the mixture by adding to their regular mixture a little of the grain the pigeons seem to prefer.

Feed only as much grain as the pigeons will clean up at each feeding. Never allow grain to lie on the floor and become moldy or you will end up with sickness in your flock. If any grain remains on the floor at the next feeding time, cut down on the amount being fed to the flock.

A small trough placed on the floor of the pen may be used as a feeder. Common four foot galvanized chick feeders with wire or reel tops make sensible pigeon feeders. When troughs are used pigeons are fed twice daily the same as if they were fed on the floor.

Fanciers with 25 to 50 pigeons may want to use better equipment. A loft this size is usually divided into two or three pens. Here trough feeders may be used, either in the center of the pen or placed on the back aisle of the pigeon house. Feeding is done each day, morning and evening.

Aisle feeders are very handy where several pens must be fed. They are filled from the aisle at the front or back of the house. The attendant need not enter the pens or disturb the pigeons.

Commercial lofts, where large numbers of birds are housed, almost always use the cafeteria system of feed, or provide aisle troughs. Since the time element is important in caring for large numbers of pigeons, the cafeteria system is recommended. Cafeteria feeders are filled once each week.

Prepared Feed or Home Mixed Ration

The individual with only a few pigeons cannot afford to mix his or her own rations. Unless the different grains can be bought in quantities of 100 pounds or more of each grain at a time, there is no saving in mixing your own feed.

Many larger feed companies sell a ready mixed all-grain pigeon feed. This is a complete feed and should be fed just as it comes from the sack.

Some companies also sell an all-grain mixture without corn. The fancier then adds a like amount of corn to the mixture, ending up with 200 pounds of mixed feed. Since corn is usually much cheaper than the cornless pigeon mixture, this reduces the cost of the total mixture. I have known breeders to mix 25 pounds of peas with 100 pounds of mixed poultry scratch feed. This makes a fair mixture for pigeons, although not as good as the regular pigeon feeds.

Pellets are made by most pigeon feed manufacturers. But fanciers can save by using turkey pellets, hog pellets, or game bird pellets. Each of these work, and the price is considerably less. Turkey pellets are generally fresh and cheap because the feed store lot rotates quickly. I have heard of racing pigeon people who will feed dog food or even cat food with the intention of raising the protein level, but I would not recommend this.

The larger breeders housing several hundred pairs or more may save on feed costs if they buy each kind of grain separately. They then mix their own ration or feeds cafeteria style.

HOME MIXED RATIONS

NORTHERN STATES		SOUTHERN STATES	
Winter Months		*Winter Months*	
Yellow Corn	50%	Yellow Corn	40%
Peas	20%	Peas	20%
Wheat	15%	Wheat	25%
Kaffir or Milo	15%	Kaffir or Milo	15%
NORTHERN STATES		SOUTHERN STATES	
Summer Months		*Summer Months*	
Yellow Corn	25%	Yellow Corn	20%
Peas	25%	Peas	25%
Wheat	30%	Wheat	35%
Kaffir or Milo	20%	Kaffir or Milo	20%

As you feed pigeons from day to day you will observe the consumption of grain varies according to temperatures, seasons of the year, and condition of the birds. My pigeons consume more corn during the cold winter months. With the approach of spring and warm weather, they slack off the corn and eat more milo and wheat. During the moulting season when they are growing new feathers, they need more protein and will eat more peas.

No mixture of grain is perfect, nor will it fit all seasons of the year. But if you watch your pigeons, they will soon tell you whether you are feeding too much or too little of any one grain. For instance, if each day they clean up the corn first and leave the peas, add a little corn to the next day's feeding, cut down a little on the peas. The sensible rule to follow is to cut down a little on anything they are leaving, add a little of those grains they clean up first.

Cafeteria Feeding

You can use the cafeteria style of feeding with a divided self feeder. Each kind of grain is available from a separate compartment. This systems has many advantages listed as follows:

SAVES TIME. The feeders are filled weekly. This saves many hours of labor weekly when compared to the twice daily system of feeding. The caretaker may be away from the loft for a day or more at a time without the pigeons missing a meal.

FEED COST IS LOWER. Feed is one of the largest costs in larger squab plants. Corn, wheat, kaffir, and peas may be bought in bulk quantities much cheaper than ready-mixed feed. Cafeteria feeding enables you to use home grown grains, which are always lowest in price.

PIGEONS BALANCE OWN RATION. You banish the worry of whether you are feeding too much or too little of any one grain. Pigeons eat the kind of grain they need to stay healthy and reproduce.

In years past when Foy Pigeon Farm was in operation several thousand pigeons were fed cafeteria style. This method was used for years and was an unparalleled system for feeding a large number of breeders.

Good feeders are constructed so mice cannot hide under them. Each feeder has a platform 12 inches wide at the front. Any kernel of grain accidentally falling from the feeder will lodge on this platform to be picked up immediately by other birds, and waste is prevented.

The bottom of each compartment should be raked out once a week. This removes chaff, husks, dust, and bits of debris that naturally work down to the bottom of the feeder. Cafeteria feeders will not work if each compartment is filled with mixed grains. To insure success each compartment must be filled with only one kind of grain. As good as cafeteria feeders sound, they have one big drawback. The feed is available day and night. So you may find yourself feeding mice.

Pigeon Grit (Mineral Mixture)

Pigeons in confinement cannot get the salts and minerals they need from their grain . . . so a mineral mixture must be provided for them. This is called pigeon grit. It is not a simple mixture of oyster shell and crushed granite grit such as is used for chickens. SUCH A MIXTURE IS WHOLLY INADEQUATE FOR PIGEONS. A complete mineral for pigeons should include salt, iodine, trace minerals, sulphur, iron, bonemeal, charcoal, and other ingredients along with the shell and granite.

Salt is one of the most important of these minerals. No bird or animal will remain healthy and raise young without salt. Yet, too much salt will poison a pigeon. A good mixture contains just the right proportion. A small amount of sulphur in the mixture is a deterrent to pigeon pox. Charcoal sweetens the crop and offsets the effects of any moldy kernel of grain the pigeon might pick up.

Iron is a blood builder and tonic, bonemeal aids in the development of bone structure. Iodine and trace minerals are all needed.

A working pair of pigeons feeding their squabs to four weeks of age will consume 5 to 7 pounds of pigeon grit a year. Do not neglect this item, though it may be a small one. Remember, a good mineral mixture is JUST AS IMPORTANT AS GOOD FEED in contributing to the health of your pigeons.

Are your pigeons slipping? Perhaps they need grit

Beginners often need advice when they encounter problems raising their squabs. Perhaps the pigeons they bought six months or a year previously had worked faithfully, produced squabs right from the beginning. Then in a few months the birds began a gradual decline. The squabs grew smaller. More and more squabs were lost before weaning time. Finally, production was down by

Squabs just hatched. The larger squab is two days old, the small squab has just hatched.

50%, and the pigeon raiser sensed something was wrong and asked for help.

What was their trouble? Three times out of four we found them feeding no grit at all, or perhaps only oyster shells. As soon as their pigeons were provided an adequate mineral mixture and were given time to replenish their mineral depleted bodies, squab production jumped back to normal.

Ready Mixed Pigeon Grit

This type of pigeon mineral comes to you ready-mixed and is fed just as it comes from the bag. Grit is not a costly item because a pair of pigeons will only eat five to six pounds of grit a year. Feed stores that sell a good volume of pigeon feed also typically sell a complete mixed pigeon mineral. There are several tested and reliable grit mixtures on the market.

Make certain the mineral mixture you buy is one made ESPECIALLY FOR PIGEONS. A really good pigeon mineral should contain eight or more ingredients. Granite grit or oyster shell alone, or a mixture of the two is not enough to meet your pigeons' mineral requirements.

Many feed companies now offer pigeon feed in pellet form. To prepare it, all the different grains are ground, mixed together, and salt and other minerals are added. The mixture is then compressed in a special pellet machine, emerging as a complete pellet feed for your pigeons.

Usually, it is not necessary to provide extra grit when pigeons are on an all-pellet diet. If a mixture of part pellets, part grain is being fed, then extra grit should be made available on the side.

Pigeon Grit Concentrate

A number of pigeon fanciers live in parts of the country where pigeon grit is not available. This poses a real problem since a balanced mineral mixture is just as important to the health of the flock as feed or water.

Foy Pigeon Farm, now Foy's Pigeon Supplies, was first to market a pigeon grit concentrate. It is a mixture of the essential ingredients of a pigeon mineral supplement. The three bulky ingredients are omitted: granite grit, oyster shells, and a small amount of sand.

The fancier buys a five pound package of these essential and hard to get minerals, called pigeon grit concentrate. Simply add ninety five pounds of granite grit, oyster shell and sand, ending up with one hundred pounds of finished pigeon grit.

The advantage of using a concentrate is one of savings. Not only will you save on freight, grit mixed at home using the concentrate will cost from one third to one half the cost of factory mixed grit.

CHAPTER 6

HABITS

A pigeon is a bird of many habits. Understanding these habits will aid the fancier in caring for his or her birds. The next chapter covers management of the pigeon loft. Managing the conduct of any kind of animal or fowl requires an understanding of what it will do, what it is capable of doing, and what it cannot be expected to do. In other words, one has to know its habits.

Briefly, the pigeon hatches from the egg in seventeen days, is weaned and on its own in five to six weeks. It mates at five to six months, will raise young until it is six to ten years old, may live to be fifteen or twenty years old if it is exceptionally long lived.

MATING. Pigeons are monogamous. One male mates with only one female. The pair is a family unit, both divide the duties of hatching the eggs and feeding the young. No polygamous arrangement would work. Once mated, pigeons keep their same mate for life. Seldom will a well-mated pair break up, especially if only mated pairs are kept in the breeding pen. An unmated cock or hen in the pen with the breeders might split up a mated pair.

If one member of a mated pair dies, the remaining pigeon will soon take a new mate if one is available. Should a pigeon become sick or go out of condition, the remaining one of the pair may take another mate.

If a mate of the opposite sex is not available, cocks will sometimes mate with cocks, or hens with hens. Such matings often confuse the beginner with pigeons. If cocks mate no eggs are produced. Neither will occupy the nest at night. Mated hens often lay four eggs in the same nest which are seldom fertile unless such hens have accepted the service of a philandering cock. Both hens attempt to brood the eggs at night.

Preliminaries to mating. Pigeons carry on an ardent courtship before the mating stage. The cock struts before the female he is trying to impress. He distends his crop with air, drops the wing feathers, spreads his tail, coos and turns in circles before the female of his choice.

The female will walk away if not interested. Should she desire to mate she will stand erect, slightly ruffle the feathers on her neck, spread the feathers in her tail and advance quickly toward the male. Billing ensues. The cock will open his beak, the hen places her beak in his and a pumping or bobbing motion follows. Finally the hen crouches, the male mounts and the mating is completed.

Young pigeons may spend much time in courtship and mating. Old mated pairs go through the mating act with very few preliminaries.

MAKING THE NEST. Newly mated pigeons must first pick a site for their home. If nesting boxes are available the cock will select one. However, the fact that nests are ready and handy does not mean he will always pick a nest. Some pairs will nest on the floor, some in a corner or perhaps even on top of the nests.

If a nest is picked the pair might sit in it side by side, billing and cooing. At this stage nesting material is gathered and brought to the nest. The cock picks up small pieces, carries them to the hen in the box where she builds them into a round nest. At this stage the cock always carries the nesting material, and the hen arranges it.

After the eggs are laid and the cock is on the nest at mid-day, the hen may be seen to carry material to the cock who adds it to the nest. Some pairs build a large, deep, well cupped nest. Others gather together only a few bits of straw, sticks and feathers.

Driving. After the pair has mated and nest building is under way, the cock is not satisfied unless the hen is on the nest. If she leaves the nest, he will follow her, continually picking at her until she again takes to the nest. This is called driving. When the first egg is laid, driving ceases.

INCUBATION. After the first egg is laid, the hen may stand or crouch over it until the second egg arrives. Then incubation starts in earnest. The period of incubation is 17 to 18 days.

The hen is usually on the nest at night, remaining until mid-morning. The cock then takes the nest, covering the eggs until mid-afternoon. In rare instances cocks have been known to cover the eggs at night instead of the hens.

Feeding Young

Both male and female share the task of feeding the young. When squabs are very young the parents are most careful of the tiny, almost helpless babies in the nest. As the youngsters become older the parents are less careful. Parents continue feeding the young until they are fully feathered. After the young bird leaves the nest it might be fed for a few days by the cock bird while on the floor.

Companionship. Pigeons seem to like company and find contentment in the presence of others of their kind. Many pairs will live in harmony in the same house.

Once they are thoroughly settled they seldom interfere with other pairs in their own loft. Each pair tends to its own business of mating, breeding and rearing young.

When a new pair is introduced to the pen, this pair may be picked on by the older residents. Within a few days, however, the new birds are accepted as regulars and all the pairs again live in harmony.

Ownership. Pigeons display a marked sense of ownership. They recognize their nest and landing board in front of their nest as their own and will defend it against trespassing by any other pigeon. In a well-settled pen of breeders each pair lives in harmony. Fighting for possession of the nest does not occur if each pair has its own (single or double) nesting compartment. If there

In four short weeks squabs weigh more than their parents. At this age, just before they begin to fly, they are ready for weaning.

are more pairs than nests there will be trouble. If there are more nests than pairs several pairs may fight for the extra nests. Vacant nests should be closed off in the interest of loft harmony.

Location of nest. Pigeons have a well developed sense of location. They will fly unerringly to their particular niche although it is identical in everything except location with every other nest in the loft.

NESTING BEHAVIOR. The pigeon's actions are guided entirely by instinct or by the cycle of its body functions. This is why a barren hen will set upon a nest without eggs. She has gone through the cycle of mating, then through the cycle of laying (although unable to lay), next she broods the empty nest.

If two eggs are laid on a flat surface and roll more than a few inches apart, the hen will brood one and pay no attention to the other although it would be very easy to reach out and tuck it under her breast.

If a tiny squab falls out of a nest it might be abandoned. The parents either do not realize the baby is gone or do not recognize it as their own. If a maturing squab is separated from its parents and begs for food, it will be fed because pigeons love to feed babies.

Fear. Pigeons fear the unusual. They are easily disturbed by fire-crackers and other loud noises, as well as quick movements. Their fears are more acute at night than during daylight hours. They have to be because they are a prey animal. They will alight as a flock to reduce their individual chances of being taken by a predator.

Confinement. People who keep pigeons as pets often entertain the mistaken idea that pigeons are unhappy when confined to loft and fly-pen. Exactly the opposite is true. Pigeons are happier and feel more secure when protected by their house and pen. Birds raised in confinement are definitely unhappy when pushed into a strange world. They are afraid of everything that moves, flies or walks.

The only exceptions to this rule are Racing Homers, Rollers, Flights and other strong flying breeds. They enjoy periods of freedom, but will hurry back to the protection of their loft at the first sign of danger.

CHAPTER 7

MANAGEMENT
OF THE LOFT

If you are raising pigeons as a money-making venture or only keeping a few birds for pleasure, you will fare much better if you do the managing for them. In the previous chapter we described some of the habits of pigeons and explained oddities of behavior. The key to successful management of pigeons is to understand their habits, then apply your knowledge to direct the pigeons along the road to productivity.

Segregate Odd Birds and Youngsters

The small fancier with only a few pairs of pigeons often keeps them all in one pen with reasonable success. But absolute segregation of mated pairs from unmated pigeons is a necessity for the large breeder where efficiency of operation is important. A separate pen for non-mated adults and immature youngsters is a must in any commercial operation.

Therefore, if only mated pairs are being kept in the breeding pen, and one member of a pair dies, its mate should be removed to the odd bird pen at once. A sickly individual, not working, should be removed with its mate.

Mating Young Birds

Most breeders keep their youngsters past eight weeks of age in a young bird pen, where they may be allowed to mate of their own accord. When a young pair mates and begins to nest they should be banded for identification. Use coiled pair bandettes with bold numbers. These fit on adult pigeons. It is common practice to band males on the right leg, females on the left, the pair bearing identical numbers. This young pair may then be transferred to another pen of breeders, care being taken that a nest is provided for them and they are properly settled in it.

Because pigeons are usually ready to mate at any time, in any place and in almost any season, it is comparatively easy to improve strains by selective breeding. Many breeders force mate their youngsters to improve their stock for show or production. Fortunately most pigeons will mate just as readily with a mate their owner picks for them as with one of their own choosing.

Watch Nesting Habits

Some pairs of pigeons build a large, deep nest using plenty of material. Others gather together only a few spears of straw, making a very skimpy nest.

Ample, cup shaped nests are ideal because they prevent the eggs from rolling out. But when a pair builds an inadequate nest, the loft owner should augment it with additional material. Straw or other materials should be placed around the nest and especially in the corners, making the outer parts of the nest higher than the middle.

Because a pigeon apparently does not know enough to retrieve an egg that rolls out of the nest, a stray egg is lost. Deep nests and well-filled corners will prevent this accident.

Nest bowls are popular with breeders. These may be obtained from Foy's Pigeon Supplies. Some are permanent, some made of pulp or fibre to be used for only one clutch of squabs. Heavy plas-

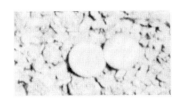

Pigeons sometimes nest right on the floor. If an egg rolls a few inches out of the nest the pigeon probably will not recover it.

tic nest bowls may be used over after cleaning. A bowl shaped nest helps prevent egg loss.

Pairs nesting on the floor or on flat surfaces present another problem. Secure such nests by enclosing them with a low two inch by twelve inch frame. Put plenty of nesting material around the sides and leave a depression in the center for the eggs. See picture below.

Surround a floor nest with a wooden frame twelve inches square, two inches high. Add nesting material around the edges until the eggs rest in a cup shaped depression. Eggs will then stay in center of nest.

Driving

The driving habit of pigeons is a sure indication of their sex. You may be positive the driving bird is male and the bird being driven is female.

Never lock a driving pair outside in the fly-pen, or in another pen without nests. A cock will peck the hen until she is scalped in his endeavor to drive her to the non-existent nest. If you plan to ship birds, each member of a driving pair should be put in a separate compartment of the crate.

Orphaned Squabs

Pigeons usually feed their young well. However, conditions may arise through death or loss where the owner must take steps to save squabs. Squabs under two weeks old may be given to another pair provided the squabs are the same size and color. Many pairs will feed three squabs as easily as two, never seeming to realize they have an adopted one in their nest. Three squabs to a nest are enough. If two squabs are to be moved, split them up, giving one each to two different pairs.

Care of Weanling Squabs

The most critical period of a squab's life is after it leaves the nest and before it has learned to eat. Such squabs pursue their parents begging to be fed. They may also chase pigeons other than their parents, only to be severely pecked and beaten by these unfriendly birds.

Some lofts have a wide board nailed to one wall of the loft to create a shelf about five inches off the floor. If a weanling squab on the floor gets into serious trouble he can beat a hasty retreat under the board where the old birds cannot pick him.

Some breeders recommend confining young birds to a small coop or pen for several weeks after weaning. Shallow pans of both feed and water are placed on the floor where these youngsters cannot help but find them. In a few weeks, they will be well accustomed to eating and drinking independently. Then they are ready to be transferred to the young bird pen.

If you are keeping young birds for future breeders, leave them in the pen with the old birds until they are at least ten weeks old, then move them to the young bird pen. In years past Frank Foy raised many pigeons for stock birds. He claimed young birds always made better progress if kept with the old ones for a month or more after weaning.

Right Number of Nests Important

Pigeons prefer to live in harmony. Each pair happily existing as a family unit respecting the rights of other pairs, but ready to fight vigorously if their home is disturbed.

The first requisite for peace and harmony in the breeding pen is that no bachelors, widows, or unattached troublemakers live in the same pen with the mated couples. Unmated individuals in the pen mean trouble and plenty of it. Keep them out.

Second, each pair should have one double nest, no more, no less. It is obvious that if there are more pairs than nests, unrest will follow. The pair without a nest will try to take one by force if necessary.

Likewise, more nests than pairs cause conflict, too. A pair of pigeons will use one nest and try to claim adjacent empty nests when possible. This is not good for the harmony in the loft since several other pairs may try to lay claim to the unoccupied nests. Unused double nests should be closed off. Each pair owning one nest only will stay at home, mind their business and give a minimum of trouble.

How to Settle New Pairs in the Loft

Each time a new pair of pigeons is introduced into the breeding loft some disorder will follow. Each older pair in the loft will try to bully the newer pair. Bickering will result from the newest pair trying to locate and settle in their new nest.

This confusion may be prevented if the new pair is locked in their new nest box for a few days. Some breeders confine the new pair to their designated nest box with a false front or a nest front with its door closed up. This plan works very well, and should be followed when a new pair is added to a settled pen.

Advantage of Identical Nests in Multiple Units

Multiple unit housing (a long coop of several pens) should be built so that each nesting unit is identical. For instance, if 20 nests are placed on the east wall in the first pen, the same number of nests should be placed in the same relative position of pen two, three, etc.

Pigeons remember the location of their nest in the loft. For example, if a pair occupying the top, right hand nest in pen three were lost or sold, the pair occupying the top, right hand nest in any of the other pens could be moved to pen three. This pair would immediately settle in the empty nest because that was the location of their nest in their former pen.

Barren Hens

Occasionally a hen will become barren because she lays too frequently, her diet is inadequate, or some accident has occurred. She will go through the motions of mating, laying, then sit on the empty nest. She may be given one or two eggs from another pair of pigeons, laid at the same time she would have had hers. She will brood the eggs and raise the squabs. Many times this is all she needs to bring her back to normal. The next time she mates the eggs will follow as they should. There is something about the rest she gets, the brooding of the eggs, feeding and rearing of the squabs that restores her to her natural breeding cycle.

Disturbances

Pigeons are upset by sudden noises or movements. Their fears are more pronounced at night than during the day. Pounding with a hammer, gun-fire, or frequent disturbances in their pen may cause them to abandon their nest.

Rats running through the house at night may bother nesting birds. A heavy infestation of lice, or a house loaded with mites may cause the brooding birds so much discomfort they will abandon their nest.

Most Breeds Should Not Fly at Large

Beginners with pigeons often write and ask how soon they should release their newly acquired pairs. They seem to imagine pigeons suffer under confinement.

Just the opposite is true. Neither the heavier breeds of utility pigeons, the ornamentals, nor the fancies are strong flyers. These types of pigeons have been raised in confinement. They know no other life. They are startled by everything that moves or flies unless they are under the protection of their house or covered fly-pen. These birds would simply not survive in the wild.

Pigeons feel safer locked within their loft and fly-pen,
knowing predators cannot reach them.

*A fly-pen allows non-race team Homers safe access
to fresh air and sunshine. Courtesy of
Clair Hetland, Minnesota.*

Pigeons Need Not be a Nuisance

Pigeons kept in a town or city may cause trouble, especially if they roost on top of a nearby house. Should the neighbors complain, you might be forced to confine your pigeons or dispose of them entirely.

Well-trained pigeons may get their exercise by flying at large during certain hours of the day, spending the rest of their time locked in their loft. A simple pigeon trap is all that is needed to make this possible.

A trap is simply a one-way door into the pigeon house. Swinging bob wires allow the pigeons to enter at will and prevent them from leaving. Stragglers homing from a race or lost birds entering the trap automatically lock themselves into your loft, regardless of the time of day they put in their appearance.

Breeders of Racing Homers, Rollers, Tipplers and other flying pigeons often exercise their birds once or twice daily. A common practice is to let the birds exercise an hour or more at night or early in the morning, about 7 or 8 a.m. Most of this time they will be on the wing. After an hour of exercise, rattle the feed pan and fill the feeders inside the house. Hungry birds will enter at once and rush for their feed. Once through the trap the pigeons are locked in and you can keep them confined the rest of the day.

If you wish, you may give your birds a second exercise period at night, but always do this just before feeding. Call the pigeons back into the house the same as before. Pigeons fly best and trap best when they are hungry. Never feed the pigeons first and then allow them to fly. Birds without incentive to come in may tarry and spend a dangerous night outside the coop. In the evening, it is wise to take measures to prevent entry into the coop by nocturnal predators. A cage or board over the trap door is a good idea. There are horror stories about inquisitive cats, cunning raccoons, ferrets and other animals which are dangerous to your flock.

Training Birds to Your Loft

If you wish to liberate your pigeons there are certain points to remember. First, the newly acquired pair should be kept inside until they have eggs or young in the nest. By that time they should consider your loft their home.

Second, give them their freedom gradually. Make an opening your birds can get through in the upper section of a wall in your loft. Put a one way trap door in the opening. Place a small eighteen or twenty-four square inch platform outside this opening as a platform and landing board. Open the hole, raise the bobs of the trap, and allow the pigeons to take their time in finding their way outside. It may be several days before they venture out.

Third, do not allow anything to frighten your pigeons when they are first outside. Everything outside is new to them. They have to learn how to get back into the house and this takes time.

A standard pigeon trap.

A frightened pigeon will fly away in any direction, and may not be able to find its way back to your loft.

Your problem is simplified if you have other, already trained pigeons flying outside. The other pigeons tend to hold the new pair around your loft and show them where and how to get in and out.

Racing Homers bought as adults from another breeder should always be held as prisoners. It is never entirely safe to release them. Their young may be allowed to fly at large and trained to return to your loft at all times. Birds raised elsewhere still regard the other loft their home. If properly trained they will fly great distances to return to it.

CHAPTER 8

DISEASES AND PARASITES

As you read this chapter on pigeon diseases you might as well face the truth—little clinical research has been done on pigeon diseases and even less has been done on pigeon medications.

The reason is economic. Should some serious disease threaten the poultry industry, scores of laboratories and agricultural colleges would begin research at once. The industry is so large that everyone would rush to find a remedy, banking on huge profits.

This is not true with pigeons. Not enough people raise them. No laboratory will spend thousands of dollars looking for a drug to cure a pigeon disease because the potential market is too small. Researchers could not get their money back if they found a specific remedy.

The few certain cures we have for pigeon diseases today were discovered primarily by accident. They were not intended for pigeons in the first place. At this point there are only four products on the market that were made and marketed with pigeons in mind. They are Carnidazole for Canker, Pigeon Pox Vaccine, Paramyxovirus Vaccine and Paratyphoid Vaccine. There are many other pigeon drugs made in Europe, but only a fraction meet U.S. FDA standards. People do sell the illegal drugs recklessly. American pigeon raisers will all suffer as a consequence, because this practice can contribute to the eventual immunity of bacteria and viruses to control by drugs.

There are many drugs legally sold in the United States that are intended for chickens and other poultry. My training as a pharmacist and my experience with pigeons has taught me, Clair

Hetland, how to use these drugs on pigeons and how to use them safely.

I keep a loft of 300 pigeons. My loft is in the city and is anything but ideal. The loft is below ground level, dark, damp, and poorly ventilated but I have solved these problems with power ventilation, gas heat, and lighting. I consider my loft to be my laboratory and I use every product sold at Foy's to see if they do any harm. Some products on the U.S. market have been tried that did do harm, for example Ren-o-sol (in the wrong dose) and wormal tablets. My birds are healthy and I successfully fly racing pigeons at the highest level with the help of many tonic products. I have pigeons worth up to $1,500 that get the same testing as the regular birds.

WHEN TROUBLE STRIKES, CHECK LOFT CONDITIONS FIRST

Pigeons are hardy animals and are naturally healthy. If given proper feed and minerals they stay healthy. Nine times out of ten if you visit a loft and find many sick pigeons present, the owner is at fault, not the pigeons.

An occasional sick pigeon in the flock is no cause for alarm. But if several get sick at once and all have the same symptoms, it is time for action. Item by item, check the following:

FEED. Does your feed contain a mixture of grains? Does it contain at least 20% peas? Is each kind of grain old, dry, sound, free from mold or mustiness of any kind?

Without peas in the ration your pigeons are only half fed. Many of the pairs will not lay, pigeons that do not die will gain slowly. New grain, moldy or musty grain could cause sour crop, vomiting, and diarrhea. Droppings of pigeons fed moldy grain will often be loose and watery.

GRIT. Do your pigeons have access to a regular pigeon mineral mixture? Oyster shell and gravel, such as is given to chickens, is not enough. Feeding of a mineral mixture to pigeons is important. Read the article on pigeon grit located in Chapter 5. If no grit is fed, many of the squabs will die before three weeks of age. They cannot live without the salts and minerals the grit provides.

WATER. Do you change the water in the pans each day? Are the pans covered so the droppings cannot contaminate the water?

Worms will live in water as will germs of Canker and other diseases. Keeping the water pan clean prevents the spread of disease from pigeon to pigeon.

DAMPNESS. Is the floor of your house dry, even close to the water fountain? Watch for wet spots on the floor or in the fly-pen. Germs of most diseases will die within a few hours if they fall on a dry surface, but will live for days in a wet spot on the floor or fly-pen.

LICE. Catch several birds, examine them for lice. Look closely next to the skin at the base of the tail and around the vent. Lice in large numbers lower the resistance of pigeons to the point the bird will catch the first disease that comes along.

MITES. These are small grayish or red bugs usually found in corners of the nests, in cracks under the roosts or cracks in the wall. They are bloodsuckers and will quickly lower the vitality of pigeons.

Diagnosis—Locating the Trouble

Diseases of pigeons usually fall into three classes:

DISEASES OF THE RESPIRATORY TRACT. These include most colds. If the pigeon coughs, sneezes or rattles when it breathes, you can be certain the trouble is in the lungs or throat.

DISEASES OF THE DIGESTIVE TRACT. These are many, including: poisoning, diarrhea, worm infestation, and sour crop. Vomiting is one symptom of digestive trouble, as are loose, watery droppings or green staining of the feathers around the vent.

DISEASES OF ORGANS AND OTHERS. Except for the One Eye Colds, these diseases can appear anywhere on the body: Pox and Canker.

Canker

Canker is caused by the protozoa *Trichomonas Columbae*. This organism is readily seen under a low power microscope. It is found in domestic and wild pigeons and doves in all parts of the world.

It is spread by contact between pigeons, such as billing, mating and feeding young. The causative organism will live for some time in water or in damp spots on the floor or fly-pen.

Older pigeons are more resistant to Canker than young. When older birds are infected they usually show a small sore on the lip or in the corner of the mouth. Yellowish patches of cheese-like material may form in the roof of the mouth. Navel Canker never attacks old birds.

Pigeons do not always show signs of Canker in the mouth even when they have Canker. Savvy fanciers have purchased top show birds because the seller felt the bird would not breed. The buyer would take the bird home, treat it for Canker and the bird would turn around and breed well. Most pigeon fanciers will treat their flocks for Canker prior to the breeding season and at the end of the breeding season. Of course, whenever symptoms of Canker occur the birds must be treated.

Squabs are highly susceptible to Canker. Common symptoms are patches of yellow cheese-like growth in the roof of the mouth and throat. This may grow so large as to prevent the passage of food and the squab will eventually starve or choke to death.

A sore and inflamed navel is also a sign of Canker. At times the whole abdomen cements together in a hard, inflamed mass.

Infected squabs indicate that the entire flock should be treated for Canker. If a squab has Canker it had to get it from the parent and the parent used the communal water fountain, etc., etc. Treatments for Canker change often. Medications that were helpful have been banned by the Food and Drug Administration mostly because they were heavily used to treat hogs illegally. But various products are generally available. Foy's catalog gives up to date remedies. If the pigeon fails to respond to Canker medication, you can assume that Canker is not the cause of their illness.

Pigeon Pox

Pigeon Pox is caused by a virus. It is found in all parts of the United States, but is common in the South. It is not spread through the droppings. The most common source of infection is bloodsucking parasites, such as the mosquito, mite, and bedbug. These bugs act as intermediate hosts, carrying the disease from pigeon to pigeon. The virus can be spread by contact, and will live for days in the drinking water. The diptheric type which attacks the throat is most common in the northern states. Symptoms to look for are yellowish patches in the throat of infected birds. Since both Canker and Pox look a great deal alike, any pigeon which has been treated for Canker and does not respond to medication should be suspected of Pox.

The outward type of Pox affects the skin and head. Small blisters often appear around the eyes or on the face. These enlarge, later become festered, then scab over. When young squabs are infected, they may show brownish patches over the body after dressing.

Once a pigeon has had Pox and recovered it will be immune for life.

The best preventive is vaccination. Pigeon Pox vaccine is inexpensive and easy to administer. Pluck a few feathers from the pigeon's thigh and rub the vaccine into the opening in the skin.

Since biting insects are carriers, the pigeon house should be sprayed with any insecticide available from your feed or garden supply store. DDT, Lindane, and Rotenone were available before it was known their use was detrimental to the ecology. It is best to buy insecticides from a pigeon supply house, especially since we at Foy's test all products on our birds.

Insect strips work well at first, but become covered with feather dust from the pigeons. The dust acts as a seal and will prevent strips from releasing their insecticide. You can carefully rinse them off from time to time with warm soap and water. Be sure to wear rubber gloves. One fancier would put twelve Vapona strips in a gallon jar. He would leave the jar open for an hour a day, generally at dusk, then seal it up until the next night. This is a great method for controlling mosquitoes and flies. As an added bonus, they will kill lice on the pigeons and drive out mites and other insects. You will find a few of these strips hung in the loft during insect weather to be good insurance against the spread of Pox.

Paratyphoid

Paratyphoid is a deadly killer of pigeons and also one of the most difficult diseases to recognize in the flock. A swollen, feverish lump on the wing or knee joint is an almost positive symptom in old birds. The swelling subsides but will leave the pigeon lame or with a dragging, stiff or useless wing. During an outbreak there may be a marked decrease in the fertility of eggs as well as many partially or fully developed squabs that die in the shell.

Affected squabs in the nest will refuse to eat, lose weight, and seem to dry up. The parents might quit feeding them. Slight diarrhea might be present. In advanced stages the neck might twist. Squabs out of the nest ruffle up, only the feathers seem to grow. They lose their appetite, stagger, appear glassy-eyed, shrivel up and die.

Until a few years ago there was no drug on the market to fight Paratyphoid in pigeons. We just had to "live with it," hoping the disease would not show up the next breeding season.

Fortunately we now have several things we can do to control Paratyphoid. If you have an outbreak you should immediately stop breeding by separating males and females. There are a variety of medications available. At this time, drugs proven to work include Cipro, Baytril, Sulfa-trimethhoprim, Albon, Sulmet, and Aureomycin. Whether these drugs will be the best in five years we don't know. Check with Foy's or your veterinarian.

It is best to prevent Paratyphoid by vaccination. This vaccine does a good job only when directions are followed.

Another prevention is to acidify the litter. A combination of Sodium Acid Sulfate and Sulfur applied to the floor will work well. It should be noted that lime is alkaline and when used it will PROMOTE Paratyphoid. A tablespoon of vinegar per gallon of drinking water will help control Salmonella from being spread in the water. Of course, keeping droppings out of the drinking water is essential.

It should be noted that doves do not live long if they get Paratyphoid. So if you keep a pair of doves in your loft and they do okay you probably do not have Paratyphoid.

The insidious part of the disease is the difficulty of completely eliminating it. You can cure 95% of your flock and be left with 5% that also survived, but have become carriers. Finding those birds can be difficult. If you have a pair that survived an outbreak but still loses babies you must cull them.

At the time of this writing, it is my understanding that Baytril, Sarafloxin, and Cipro will remove the disease from carriers. But I am willing to bet that that won't last because these drugs are being used recklessly. The Paratyphoid bacteria will build up an immunity to these medications due to irresponsible distribution. These drugs should only be obtained from a veterinarian and then only used according to the prescription instructions.

Sour Crop

Sour crop is caused by moldy, soured, or heated grain, by filthy water or by feeding anything that has spoiled, soured or become moldy. Sick birds frequently vomit partially digested grain. This is picked up by others in the loft who in turn become sick and vomit. Soon a large number of birds are affected.

Some birds become too full or too weak to vomit, and the grain stays in the crop, which will soon become greatly extended with food and water. Feed and liquids worked from the crop will have a distinctly sour smell.

Should sour crop appear, examine the feed at once for mold or spoilage. Remove all sick birds from the pen. Withhold all feed from sick birds for a day, then feed sparingly until they have recovered.

If the crop of a sick pigeon is filled with grain and fluids, hold the pigeon's head downward and gently work the contents out of the crop. This is a delicate procedure, because the birds are in a weakened condition and can be frail. Wash out the crop with an infants' syringe, using a teaspoon of baking soda to a pint of warm water.

E-Coli

Symptoms and treatments are very similar to those for Paratyphoid. Two drugs that seem to help are Vetisulid and Apralan. There is no vaccine for E-Coli, but having the birds vaccinated for Salmonella will help to some extent.

Colds

Colds in the loft indicate an overall low vitality and poor resistance. An unbalanced grain ration, a lack of grit, birds heavily infested with lice, mites or worms—any of these may increase the flock's susceptibility to disease. Drafty houses, wet floors or crowding may also be blamed.

The surest signs of a cold are watering eyes and a slight discharge from the nostrils. The birds lose weight and sit around with feathers ruffled.

Good care will speed recovery. Make certain your pigeons do not roost in a draft between open windows. Feed a balanced grain mixture containing peas. Make certain they have access to a proper mineral mixture (pigeon grit). Also, confine sick birds to a warm, dry pen.

Treat colds by giving one or two Aureomycin 25mg tablets twice a day for three to five days. Then follow them with one Cod Liver Oil capsule a day for a few days or a no-lite tablet daily for several days or both. Watch birds after giving an Aureomycin tablet because they often throw them up. If they do, just give it to them again. You might need to break up the tablet.

To treat a flock of pigeons you can use Gallimycin, Spectinomycin, or Tylan. Tylan is generally given with Aureomycin. One of these three may work for one outbreak and not for another. Again, I must say that drugs come and go so best to check with Foy's.

Chronic Colds—Bronchitis—Coryza

This chronic respiratory condition in pigeons, known by several names, is commonly found in pigeons in all parts of the United States.

There are certain symptoms to look for—a harsh cough or rattle in the throat which persists for many weeks. The affected bird may breathe heavily or rattle in the chest when disturbed. It may stand in the corner, gasping for air. If you hold a sick bird close to your ear you will be able to hear a distinct, crackling noise in its lungs. If you were to conduct a post mortem you would see the walls of its windpipe thickened and inflamed. Many affected birds die. Others continue to work, eat, raise young and may eventually recover. Good care and feeding, a balanced grain diet, and an adequate mineral mixture seem to help keep the disease in check.

Until recently the only treatment we knew was to inject an antibiotic into the flesh of the bird using a hypodermic needle.

This was a risky procedure at best, sometimes as many birds were killed as were cured.

You can mark on your calender when to expect respiratory disease—July. This is often because your loft has become overcrowded. It is not unusual for a breeder to start the season with 30 pairs of breeders and end up with 200 birds in July. Packed lofts with hot days and cool nights and bingo!—you have rattles. So next year treat the birds for respiratory disease July 1. If you go into the loft at night and listen you will hear birds sneezing. If you don't hear sneezing, don't medicate.

To treat a flock of pigeons there are three products on the market that work well. The most effective medicine is Gallimycin, the next best is Tylan, and then LS 50. Although none of these drugs are indicated for pigeons all do work very well. The manufacturer has no indications for pigeons but very few products have those indications.

One Eye Colds

This is not a true cold, and should be classified as an eye infection. It is more common in squabs than in adults.

The first symptom is watering of the eye. This discharge will thicken and the feathers around the eye may become matted together with a yellow fluid.

Terramycin Sore Eye Ointment applied directly to the eye can be helpful. It is a good idea to fill the cleft in the roof of the mouth with this ointment at the same time you treat the eye because in the pigeon, the eye and the nose are usually involved at the same time.

I give two Aureomycin 25 tablets twice a day for three to five days while birds have this eye infection. Many times what appears to be an eye cold will simply be the result of irritation in the roof of the mouth. This is very common in short-faced breeds. If you have many birds with one eye colds you must be careful—you may have an ornithosis outbreak, and you yourself can get this disease. If birds have ornithosis you need to treat with a heavy dose of a tetracycline for 30 to 45 days. It's much easier to treat this disease in people.

Paramyxovirus

Paramyxovirus is closely related to Newcastles disease, but pigeons don't get Newcastles and chickens don't get Paramyxovirus.

This virus is spread by direct contact. By wind, by dust (on feedsacks), and by humans.

Pigeons will become thirsty and their droppings will be wet, the floor looks as if you poured water on it. Birds appear dizzy - some hold their heads upside down, some become paralyzed in the legs. The birds have trouble eating, pecking at food and missing it.

What to do? Vaccinate to prevent it. If you already have it, vaccinate all that you have. It will take three weeks to establish immunity. Give the electrolytes as the loose droppings will deplete electrolytes. Shortage of electrolytes will cause death. We also recommend using Albon for nine days. This drug has no effect on the virus but will help the birds fight off other diseases that may take a hold when the bird is sick. Outbreaks vary. It is well worth your effort to try to pull birds through.

After an outbreak is over do not raise any young for a month or two. The virus will not survive outside the pigeon loft.

Care and of Beaks and Toenails

Occasionally both beaks and toenails must be trimmed on some pigeons in your loft. A slightly crossed beak may be corrected by trimming. Long hooked (or "hawk-beaked") upper bills should be trimmed back. Upper beaks on some breeds such as Tumblers and Turbits often need attention. The ideal instrument for cutting beaks and toenails is a small fingernail clipper. Also trim long toenails, using the same kind of clipper.

Internal Parasites

ROUND WORM. This is the worm most often found in pigeons. It is one-half to one and one-half inches long, about the thickness of a piece of common white string.

TAPE WORMS. These are not often found in pigeons. The worm is white, flat rather than round, and jointed. Usually the head is fastened to the wall of the intestine. May be from one-half to three or more inches long.

HAIR WORMS. These are very small, about as thick as a hair, are usually tightly coiled when seen. Because of their very small size they are often overlooked by the average person. You may discover them by washing out the contents of a slit intestine in a pan of water, then slowly pour off the water down to the last few drops. Worms will be seen on the bottom of the pan.

In order to check for worms of any kind you must kill a bird suspected of harboring them, then slit its intestine from end to end. If present, worms are readily seen. Tape worms are flat, segmented (jointed) may be several inches long. Round worms look like short pieces of white string. Hair worms are about the thickness of a hair, are usually tightly coiled. Worms lay their eggs inside the intestines of the pigeon. These then pass out through the droppings onto the ground. Another pigeon picks up the eggs, and will become infested.

   Good sanitation is the best way to prevent worms. Feeders, grit feeders and water fountains should be covered to avoid contamination by droppings. A wire bottomed fly-pen is excellent to prevent the spread of worms since droppings go right on through. Worm eggs live in moist soil or damp floor coverings. Litter in the house should be dry.

TREATMENT. The control of worms in pigeons is now much easier than in the past. New drugs have been developed which can be used in the drinking water, and these make worming an easy task.

Use Piperazine wormer in the drinking water to rid your birds of the infestations from the roundworm family (Ascarids), which are the most common type of pigeon worm. Birds may reinfest themselves so treatment should be repeated in 30 days.

There are special wormers available for tapeworms or hair-worms (Capillaria). Foy's will either have these drugs or let you know how to get them.

External Parasites

Feather Louse. This small, dark louse is common to all pigeons. Slightly thicker than a hair, it is one-eighth to one-fourth of an inch long. It is easily seen on the large wing feathers of the pigeon, often tightly fastened close to the feather shaft or sticking to the outer body of the feather. Other than eating small holes in the feather, this louse apparently does not harm the pigeon.

Body Lice. There are several species of body louse, ranging from yellow to brown in color. They are easily seen when you ruffle back the feathers around the vent and at the base of the tail around the oil gland. Examination for lice should be made in bright daylight. The lice will be seen scurrying for cover when exposed.

Body lice are not bloodsuckers, but heavily infested pigeons are nervous and uncomfortable. Lice in large numbers will definitely lower the vitality of your flock and should be considered a menace to a pigeon's health.

Lice of all kinds may be kept under control by using a type of Permethrin insecticide. A common trade name for this product is Ectiban. There are several different applications of Ectiban. The Ectiban dust can be sprinkled directly on the birds. You should also be sure to dust in the nest boxes and into the nest. Or you can opt to spray the loft with Ectiban Wettable Powder. Spray everywhere and allow to dry into a powder. Do this every thirty days in warm weather. You can also spray the birds directly with Scalex Lice Spray, which is basically the same insecticide as Permethrin. Vapona Strips will help control flying insects.

Red Mite. This mite is commonly found in poultry houses. Nests of sparrows are often loaded with them. The mite will be gray or red if it is filled with blood. It is about as large as the head of a pin. The mite does not stay on the body of the pigeon. It hides during the day in cracks in the walls, in corners of the nest, and under roosts. It attacks the roosting pigeons during the night, biting and sucking their blood. It may be carried to your loft by rats or sparrows.

The mite breathes through its skin, so contact with oil of any kind will kill it. An effective old time treatment was to paint walls, nests, roosts and perches with a mixture of one-half crankcase oil and one-half kerosene. This was applied to all surfaces with a paint brush.

Malathion is an effective way to control both mites and lice in the pigeon house. Use a 50% concentrate and mix one part concentrate to 50 parts of water. This makes a 1% solution which should be sprayed on ceiling, walls, nests, and roosts. If a little of the solution falls on the pigeons it will do no harm, but it will kill all their lice.

Bedbugs. Bedbugs are seldom a problem in the pigeon house. Once a house is infested, however, they are the most difficult of all bugs to destroy. They hide in cracks and crevices the same as mites, sucking the blood of both squabs and adults when they emerge from their hiding places at night.

One method of control is to spray with Ectiban EC. Walls, ceiling, cracks in the walls and around the roosts and nests should be soaked thoroughly.

Pigeon Fly. This fly is found only in the southern half of the United States. It is possible to see these in the northern states during warm weather if they were shipped in on pigeons from the

South. The winter weather kills it, and it will not live from year to year in northern climates.

The pigeon fly is the size of and resembles an ordinary house fly. One may be seen occasionally on a pigeon, but it quickly slides under the feathers. It is a biting insect, its presence causes discomfort and nervousness in the pigeons.

The pigeon fly is resistant to many insecticides. Ectiban will kill it quickly. Pigeons may be dusted with Ectiban powder, or the house may be sprayed with a Ectiban Wettable Powder.

The adult pigeon fly will scatter hundreds of its eggs throughout the pigeon house. In three to four weeks a new crop of flies hatch out. The newest method of control is to hang insect strips in the pigeon house. These slowly emit a compound deadly to all flying insects. As the pigeon fly hatches out it is killed before it has a chance to lay its eggs. Insect strips remain effective for about three months.

Mosquitoes. The common mosquito may be a source of trouble in your loft, since it is thought to spread the virus of Pigeon Pox from pigeon to pigeon. The best control method is to spray the interior of your house as described earlier in this chapter.

Sparrows. Sparrows should not be allowed in the pigeon loft. Although they do no harm outside of the feed they eat, they may carry mites and body lice. You cannot keep a loft free of parasites if the sparrows use it freely. Screening the fly-pen with one inch mesh poultry netting will keep out sparrows.

Rats often become a serious problem. They waste and destroy feed, kill squabs and even old birds. Measures must be taken to secure the coop. Solid cement or tight wooden floors and a fly-pen screened with one inch mesh poultry netting will keep them out. There are also rat traps available.

Mice are not easy to control. If present in large numbers, they often chew the wings and tail feathers of nesting birds. A good cat is a great help. A kitten raised with and taught respect for the pigeons will not harm them, and will keep the mouse population down. Good mousetraps are readily available. Outbreaks of Paratyphoid often are traced to feed contaminated by rats and mice.

Drugs and Methods used to Control Parasites

Dipping

I use two gallons of warm water. Then I add a cup of Foy's Bath Salts and 1/2 cup of Ivomec sheep drench. Pick a warm sunny day. Dip each bird in this solution. Birds relax and seem to enjoy the dipping. They won't be able to fly because they are too wet. I save this dip solution and use it for bath water. It's too much for me to dip all birds. So I dip the pairs in individual pens and use the dip solution for the loose birds to bathe in.

Permethrin

Permethrin comes in a concentrate solution called Ectiban EC. A wettable powder called Ectiban WP and a dusting powder called Ectiban D. Permethrin is a synthetic Pyrethrin. Pyrethrin is a naturally occurring insecticide derived from a plant. The Pyrethrin products kill coldblooded creatures like insects and fish so be careful when you use and dispose of these products.

The Ectiban EC and the Ectiban WP should be sprayed with the birds out but many spray the birds. I do not recommend this but I know it is done.

Ectiban WP is sprayed throughout the loft. It dries to powder and lasts 30 days. At this writing it works against pigeon flies.

Ectiban D must be dusted on each bird.

Malathion is still available. It is a potent insecticide, and was the main ingredient in Roost Paint. You could make your own

Roost Paint by mixing two tablespoonfuls of 55% Malathion to a pint of Aromatic Spirits (Paint thinner) and shake well.

Scalex Spray is a natural Pyrethrin. It is a very safe product. You can soak birds down with it. It seems to sparkle up the feathers as well. Scalex Spray is not an aerosol, it is a pump spray. We once had aerosol sprays but found it took the bloom off the feathers. Birds would not shed water so they could not fly in even a misty rain.

CHAPTER 9

COMMERCIAL
PIGEON RAISING

The Hobbyist

Ninety percent of the pigeons raised in the United States are kept without thought of monetary profit. Some keep their pigeons to show, carefully mating outstanding individuals which may raise a prize winner for next year's pigeon show. Such fanciers may spend five dollars, twenty-five or fifty dollars for a single bird. Money is no object in the pursuit of their hobby.

Men and women, boys and girls of all ages make up a much larger group. These people like pigeons, don't care particularly whether they are show, utility or ornamental stock.

Caring for pigeons or any live animal is an education in itself, one that can not be learned from a book. Young folks develop a sense of responsibility when they realize the very life and well-being of their pets is in the hands of the one who feeds them.

Parents often buy their boy or girl a pair of pigeons, knowing that a child with something to care for develops habits of regularity and consideration for others dependent on him. Regular chores have kept many a child out of mischief.

All these people who make up the majority of pigeon raisers never think of the small expense involved. Their profit is in the joy of showing, in the pleasure of caring for something alive.

Backyard Squab operation. Courtesy of Harold Wong,
Bloomington, Minnesota.

The Small Breeder

Many fanciers start out with just a pair or two of pigeons. As time passed, these same people found themselves with several breeds, more loft room, and 25, 50 or perhaps more pairs of pigeons.

Since a fancier with 25 or more pairs of pigeons incurs a substantial feed bill in a year's time, he or she should find some means of defraying part of the cost.

These fanciers may:

1. Develop a home market for dressed squabs.

2. Hold their youngsters to mating age and sell the young mated pairs to other breeders.

If you live in a city of fair size, ten to fifteen thousand or more, it is not difficult to find customers for a few pairs of squabs each week. A surprising number of people will buy a pair or two of squabs for their table occasionally when they know they are available. Many small breeders, with fifty pairs or more of utility type breeders, sell all their squabs in their own home town.

In these instances squabs are killed, drawn, plucked, and sold "oven ready." Some producers kill, dress and sharp freeze their squabs in freezer (polyethylene plastic) bags, holding them in a locker or deep freeze until they have a sufficient number to sell.

Other breeders prefer to hold their young birds until fall or winter. When these mate at six to eight months of age they sell the mated pairs as breeders.

A good market for young mated pairs may be found among other pigeon fanciers in your own locality. Often a small ad in a local paper will find buyers for every mated pair you want to sell within just a few week's time.

It is possible through the sale of squabs and young pairs of breeders to pay part or all of the feed cost of the loft. What other hobby could you find that would provide as much enjoyment as raising pigeons and at the same time pay back most of the feed costs?

The Commercial Squab Plant

It is possible to make a very good living raising squabs for market. In the United States at present one firm houses more than 12,000 pairs, several keep 5,000 to 6,000 pairs or more, and a good number of smaller plants operate successfully with 1,000 pairs or more of breeders. These businesses have operated at a profit for some time and continue with the same number of breeders year in and year out.

Almost all of the larger plants are located along the Eastern seaboard in states from New Jersey to Florida, although there are a few in California.

Hundreds of pigeon farms start up, only to quit or fail after a few seasons. Successful plants have a few things in common:

1. The owners of the plants are thoroughly versed in pigeon husbandry. They are not beginners. Through the years they have learned every habit, every peculiarity of social behavior, and every disease of pigeons. Every pair of pigeons must be a working pair, and the owners know how to keep them producing.

2. The climate is favorable. Most plants are located in the southern half of the United States near the coast line or in a state where the temperature seldom falls below freezing. Automatic water systems may be used the whole year through. Although pigeons breed in any climate they usually slow down or quit entirely in severe freezing weather. Pigeons raise young the year around in a mild climate—that is the place to make money in the squab business.

3. Nearness to market increases profits. Squabs are bought most readily in larger cities, in resort areas, by four star hotels. The two largest markets are New York City, Florida, the larger cities located between these two points are also good markets.

Delivering squabs to the consumer is a big expense. That is why most large squab plants are located near the natural market. California has its natural market too, and there are thriving squab plants in that state to take care of it.

Larger squab farms have certain advantages in this business. They will have a good, reliable inventory, they can freeze and store squabs to wait for higher market values, they can utilize cheap labor in some areas, and they can pursue profitable side ventures only remotely connected with pigeons.

This book is not written to encourage or discourage the prospective squab raiser. To be successful in this business, you must not be afraid of work, you must have a fair amount of capital, you must pick a favorable section of the country in which to locate, and above all, you must have a thorough knowledge of the science of pigeon breeding.

CHAPTER 10

KILLING AND DRESSING SQUABS

Squabs are ready for killing when they are about four weeks old, give or take a few days either way. The best indication of the time to kill is the feathering on the side of the body under the wings. When the feathers have developed at this spot the squab is ready.

If the squab is killed too young, there will be many pinfeathers in the skin which are hard to remove and which spoil the looks of the dressed squab.

If the squab is allowed to grow too old and has started to fly, the muscles harden and the meat is no longer as tender as when the squab was still in the nest.

The best method of killing is to stick the squab with a sharp killing knife or pocket knife. Open the mouth, push the point of the knife through the roof of the mouth into the brain, give the knife a turn or twist and withdraw. The squab dies quickly and will bleed freely. Place the bleeding squab in a funnel made of tin so it cannot flop around. It should bleed for two to three minutes, and is then ready to pick.

Always pluck a squab dry. As soon as it has stopped kicking, begin picking the feathers. Rest the squab on your lap or on a table and remove all feathers except those on the head. A good picker will hold the squab by the tail feathers and the wing flights during the entire plucking to prevent blood blisters or bruises on the flesh. Be sure to remove all small feathers at the vent, the edges of the wings, and also on the hips. Don't send a squab to

The squab on the left shows pinfeathers on its body under the wing, and it is not quite old enough for market. On the right, the same squab a few days later, now fully feathered under wings, and ready for market.

market with a lot of pin feathers or you will be graded down on quality.

When you have finished removing feathers you should throw the squab in a pail of ice water so it will cool. If many squabs are being cooled it is well to have two sets of pails or tubs, removing the partly cooled squabs to the second cooling water as others are picked. Wash off all manure and blood. If squabs have feed in the crop, this must be removed. Remove feed by holding the squab, mouth open, under a running faucet. Fill the crop and shake the squab so the water and feed will come out together at the mouth. Never cut open a crop to remove grain as it spoils the looks of the squab. Three hours in cold, icy water is sufficient for cooling. If squabs are not removed when cooled they will become water-soaked and later they will be very soft. A squab properly cooled is firm and stiff and will remain so for several days.

Packing squabs for shipment to market is easily done, but is very often done incorrectly. Use a tight box, tub, pail, barrel, or other clean container. If the container is water tight, drive a nail through the bottom in several places. This allows the melting ice to drain. Line the container with newspapers or other papers and be sure the paper that comes in contact with the squabs and ice is a clean, heavy, waterproof paper. The more paper used in lining a box the slower the ice will melt. Put a thin layer of chipped ice in the bottom of the container. On this layer pack in your squabs with their heads down. When you have the bottom layer of squabs in, you should sift some chipped ice between the outside squabs and the paper lining. On top of the layer of squabs fill in with chipped ice until nothing but the squabs' feet can be seen. Place another layer of squabs in the container, followed with a layer of ice, and continue this until the box is nearly full. Place a heavy layer of coarsely chipped ice on top and then cover with several layers of paper. Use more ice and larger chips in summer than in winter.

When squabs are shipped to the large commercial markets they are graded and paid for according to quality. Some squabs are worth much more than others. Size, quality, color and condition of the meat and the condition in which they arrive after shipment all have a lot to do with the price you will get for your squabs. It pays to exercise care in the killing, preparing, and packing of squabs for the market. Learn these details as thoroughly as you would learn the manner of raising your pigeons—seek all the advice and instructions you can get from expert squab breeders along these lines.

The first part of this chapter describes a method of killing and preparing squabs for market known as "New York Dressed." This is an old method where head and feet were left on the squab and the entrails were not removed. Even today most commission houses prefer to buy squabs dressed in this manner.

Dressing for Home Market
or your own table

Chain stores are fast changing the buying habits of the American consumer. Meat is bought ready-cut and prepackaged. Fish are cleaned, scaled, fins and insides removed before they reach the meat counter. Chickens, turkeys, even squabs are carefully picked and cleaned before being sold to the customer as "oven ready."

Whether or not you find a market for your squabs may well depend on how carefully you prepare them for your customers. Most people today don't know how to draw a squab, would not think of buying one unless it was ready to cook without extra preparation. These steps should be followed in dressing squabs for home trade:

1. Kill by sticking or removing head.
2. Bleed.
3. Pick—always pick dry—do not scald.
4. Remove entrails and crop through abdominal opening. Cut off feet.
5. Singe. Remove pinfeathers with dull knife.
6. Immerse in cold water one hour or more.
7. Squab is now ready to sell or sharp freeze.

CHAPTER 11

MISCELLANEOUS INFORMATION

1. Do not feed grain on the dirt floor of your pigeon house unless the floor is perfectly dry. If the pigeons fail to clean up all their feed each day, the grain may draw moisture from the dirt floor and become moldy.

2. Moldy or moisture swollen grain of any kind will cause trouble, usually diarrhea or sour crop. While older pigeons seldom die from spoiled grain, many squabs will be lost because they are being fed on partially digested grain direct from the crops of their parents.

3. Yellow corn is the basis of all feed. Never feed new corn unless it is thoroughly dry. You must be sure that the naturally dried shelled corn is one year old. Make it a point to feed nothing but old, sound No. 2 corn. You will be more than repaid by doing so.

Many hybrid seed corn plants in the corn belt states sell artificially dried seed corn at regular feed price. These odd-sized kernels come from the tips and butts of the ear, and they will not feed smoothly through a corn planter. A farmer would not use them as seed, even though they have been through the artificial drying process. These kernels are the same price as regular dried shelled corn, and they are the best grade of corn one can possibly get for pigeons. It will pay to check around for artificially dried corn.

4. Not more than twenty-five pairs of breeders should be kept in a pen because of the difficulty involved in keeping a close

check on each pair. If your birds are divided into small units it is much easier to know just what each pair is doing.

5. If you have any odd, unmated birds, keep them in a pen separate from your breeders. An unmated bird in a pen of breeding birds will decrease production as much as 25%. Should a bird die, remove its mate from the pen immediately.

6. Squabs should be marketed at about four weeks of age. During the fourth week the squab becomes fully feathered, and it is during this last week that the squab's flesh changes from soft fat and water to good, firm, solid meat. If squabs are killed too soon there will be quite a bit of shrinkage, and the meat will be soft and flabby. Plan to wait until the squab is feathered on its sides under the wings. The squab is ready for market when its sides are fully feathered, regardless of its weight or age.

7. One familiar with pigeons can determine sex by the looks of a bird. The male is usually larger than the female, his head is blocky and his beak is short. The female has a narrow head, her beak looks longer, she is quieter than the male, less quarrelsome and does not try to show off like the male. When birds are nesting, the female will be on the nest at night and in the forenoon while the male is on from ten or eleven o'clock until about four in the afternoon.

During billing preliminary to mating the cock opens his bill, the hen places her bill inside his. When building a nest before the eggs are laid, the cock carries the straw, the hen arranges it in the nest.

8. April, May, June, and July are the best months to save squabs for breeding stock. Squabs hatched in these months will develop during the warm summer months, molt at the proper time and be ready to go to work at the season when squabs will bring the most on the market.

9. Pigeons molt during the fall months. It takes four to six weeks for a pigeon to acquire its new feathers. Occasionally, birds will molt and nest at the same time. It is better, however, to allow your birds to take a much needed rest during the moulting period. Some breeders remove all nesting material from the loft when their birds start to molt. This hastens the molting period

and induces your whole flock to molt at once. After your birds have lost their old feathers, grown new ones and had a few weeks' rest, they are ready to go back to work again.

10. It is good to leave the youngsters you are going to save for breeders in the pen with the old birds until they are from eight to ten weeks of age. When the young birds act scrappy and have lost their squeaky voice, they can be removed from the breeding pen and put in another to shift for themselves.

11. You will get much better hatches from your pigeon eggs if you give your birds fresh bath water at least four days a week; in the winter time three days a week except on days that are severely cold or cloudy. Damp birds carry the moisture back to the nest, and keep the eggs from drying out.

12. Keep your loft as clean as possible. It is a good plan to put fresh sand and gravel in the fly-pen occasionally. Do not use lime or other strong disinfectants in the house. The birds will carry it to the nest and you will have a high percentage of loss from infertile eggs and squabs dead in the shell.

13. To insure fertility, many Fantail breeders trim the tails of their birds, cutting off part of the main tail feathers close to the body, on both male and female. The outside one-fourth of the tail on each side is removed. The upright center part of the tail, about one-half, is left intact for balance. At the same time they trim away the soft, fluffy feathers from around the vent on both birds.

The fluff around the vent on other breeds may be trimmed to help fertility. The main tail feathers need not be cut.

14. If you have a female producing infertile eggs, give her the eggs from another pair which were laid about the same time. Let her hatch and raise the squabs. Usually the next eggs this female lays will be fertile. There is something about hatching squabs and feeding them until weaning time that restores the hen's normal breeding cycle and enables her to lay fertile eggs again.

15. The first clutch of eggs laid by a young hen are often infertile.

16. Nest mates are not always male and female. 50% of the time there will be one of each sex, 25% of the time both will be males, 25% of the time both will be females.

17. Plumage color in pigeons is not the same shade or color as in wild birds. In pigeons:

a. Yellow might be better described as a light tan, cream or buff.

b. Red is not bright red like a cardinal, but a dark brown or chocolate color.

c. Blue is a grayish slate color.

d. Black is glossy black.

e. White is pure white.

A mountain racing loft and fancy loft side by side. Courtesy of Scott and Mira Perrizo, Lyons, Colorado.

CHAPTER 12

RACING HOMERS

There is so much information available about Racing Homers that one could not begin to treat the subject thoroughly in less than a fair-sized book. When our customers write us, they commonly ask how to train their youngsters. In this chapter, we will give you a few of the most elementary facts about Racing Homers. If you raise Racing Homers, you will need to find out more about your birds than what we provide here. There are subtle differences between the raising of Racing Homers and squabbing pigeons.

You can obtain very complete information on all phases of the breeding, flying, feeding, and training of Racing Homers from the book "Pigeons: Racing Homer Facts and Secrets" written by Mr. Leslie C. Swanson and described at the end of this chapter.

History of Racing Homers

Racing Homers have been used to carry messages for people for centuries. We read accounts of the ancient Roman armies using pigeons to carry military messages.

Today's Racing Homer originated from Belgium. The sport of racing pigeons spread from Belgium to other nearby countries, most notably to England. There have been pigeon clubs and pigeon races in Belgium and England for over a century. During the first World War, pigeons played an important part in carrying messages when other means of communication had been destroyed. Today, there are thousands of Racing Homer fanciers in all parts of the United States.

The Racing Homer differs from the highly domesticated squabbing breeds because it can fly hundreds of miles over unfamiliar territory back to its home loft. Scientists dispute what enables a Racing Homer to find its way home under such conditions. Nevertheless, the homing instinct is bred into these birds and, if it is physically possible, they do return home.

Importance of Good Stock

As we stated before, the homing instinct and the physical characteristics necessary to make a successful flight of hundreds of miles are bred right into the Racing Homer. If you expect the best results from your birds, you must get true Racing Homer stock. It is a mistake to think that common pigeons or mongrel stock will succeed. It takes years of careful breeding to build up the stamina, the physical characteristics, and the homing instinct essential for a bird's success.

Many people, anxious to try this fascinating sport, wisely make their start by purchasing mature Racing Homer breeding stock that has been tried and tested. Of course, it is necessary to keep these old, trained birds as "prisoners." Do not allow birds of this kind to fly at large. If given their liberty, they will immediately try to return to the home loft from which they were originally trained.

You may, however, train the youngsters raised from such stock to return to your loft at all times and under all conditions.

Training of Young Birds

Racing Homers may be kept in a loft the same as squabbing Homers with one exception: they must be flown or exercised reg-

"The Gorin Cock"

Clair Hetland
Golden Valley, MN

AU 93 118

foto: Henk Kuijlaars

"Romain"

owner:
John T. Keller
Taneytown, MD.

B.86-1008167

foto: Henk Kuijlaars

Two champion long distance Racing Homers.

Young Racing Homers entering house through trap. Courtesy of American Pigeon Journal. A trap arrangement as pictured above gives the fancier complete control over his or her flock. Aluminum bob wires swinging inward allow the pigeons to enter the house at any time. After entry, wires swing back in place to prevent the pigeons from leaving the loft.

ularly to keep them in condition and to sharpen their homing instinct. It is not necessary to allow Racing Homers to fly at large at all times. In fact, it is best not to give them that privilege. A better plan is to keep your birds confined to your loft and exercise them each morning or evening, or both.

Feed and water your birds inside the loft twice daily. They will become accustomed to getting their feed and water there and will form the habit of entering the loft immediately upon returning from a race or training flight.

Begin to train young birds when they are from two to four months of age. Birds should be flown only on clear days. Do not fly your birds in threatening weather or when fog or haze impairs good visibility. Start young birds about four or five blocks from home, and let the birds go in a "group toss" by releasing all of them at the same instant. Next, return your youngsters to the same spot and release them one at a time. Allow enough time between tosses so one bird cannot simply follow another back to the loft. Next, increase the distance from home to one mile, two miles, four miles, eight miles, fourteen miles, twenty-two miles, thirty miles, and so on. Follow the same plan, stop at the same place twice, first for a group release, then for a single toss.

It is important that you toss your birds first in a group and then singly. If your birds get into the habit of flying in a group some individuals will follow along with the others on shorter flights and will not exercise their homing instinct. When these birds are later sent out on longer flights or when they encounter bad weather, they are widely scattered and put on their own resources. Eventually the entire flock is strung out and all birds are soon out of sight of one another. If there are birds in the group that have homed simply because they flew along with the flock they will be lost. However, each bird has been singly tossed from all stations, the individual will be in the habit of using its homing instinct and will not be lost on the longer flights or on races of less favorable conditions.

There is much more information available about all phases of the sport of Racing Homers. If you are just a beginner, or if you have kept racing birds for years, it will pay you to send for Leslie C. Swanson's book, "Racing Homer Facts and Secrets." It is good for the veteran and a boon for the novice.

Racing Homer Facts and Secrets

Covers the art of flying pigeons and how to race them success-fully. Complete text on breeding, feeding, conditioning and hundreds of miscellaneous tips. Learn the little things the champion fanciers do to groom their birds. Secrets they carefully guard from the novices. All about line breeding, the widower system and tricks the masters use in getting their birds in shape.

Written by Leslie C. Swanson, veteran magazine and newspaper writer, in language simple and practical, and easy to understand. No complicated and scientific theories, nor bewildering, technical terms.

This book also has a special chapter on "How to Fly Young Birds," focusing on one phase of the sport where the novice has a chance to outperform the veterans.

NEED PIGEON SUPPLIES?

Do you need seamless or mating bands to properly identify your pigeons? How about a trap to confine your pigeons to their quarters after their exercise period?

Do you know where to buy pigeon medications, vitamins, seamless bands, pair bandettes, books, nest bowls, wood eggs, feeders or fountains? Send $2 for a complete list of pigeon supplies, write to **Foy's Pigeon Supplies** and ask for the latest pigeon supply catalog.

FOY'S PIGEON SUPPLIES
P.O. BOX 27166
GOLDEN VALLEY, MN 55427-0166

History of Foy's

Over 110 years ago Frank Foy realized he could sell birds through a nationally distributed catalog. When he worked at an incubator manufacturer in Des Moines, Iowa he began putting his little catalog of birds for sale in each incubator. From that time to now Foy's has remained in business. When Frank embarked on this venture his philosophy was to give everyone a square deal—and nothing has changed there.

As Foy's grew, the farm developed into a hatchery to raise chicks, ducklings, and pigeons for sale. Charles and Frank Foy started thousands of fanciers in pigeons with good birds and good advice. The day came when Charles finally decided to stop selling pigeons. Three problems had cropped up: real estate prices rose and he had to sell his buildings, Rail Way Express quit business, and Mr. Moen, the loft manager with a sixth sense for picking pairs, retired. The sale birds went to Leo Roscoe and Charlie put all his energy into the pigeon supply business.

Later Charles Foy took over the business and ran it until he was in his mid-70s. He then sold it to the Hetland Family who moved the business to Minnesota. The Hetland family bought Foy's in 1976 to go with the supply business they started in 1960. Charlie's energy and enthusiasm were amazing. Many people don't know that Charlie was an old time open cockpit pilot. Charlie passed away in 1995 at the age of 94. He was preceded in death by his wife, Lucille.

ACKNOWLEDGEMENTS

We wish to acknowledge these people for generously sending photographs of their champion birds and lofts:

James Abel, Kasson, Minnesota
Lothar and Barbara Beer, Lindenhurst, New Jersey
Ed Bachmann, Pontiac, Michigan
Maurice Durkee, Winnebago, Minnesota
John Delahoussaye, Cleveland, Mississippi
Ron Ewing, Kansas City, Kansas
Bob and Vida Given, St Louis Park, Minnesota
John T Keller, Tanneytown, Maryland
Edward C Loomis, Lincoln, Nebraska
Peter Mesher, Plymouth, Minnesota
Richard Nauer, Osseo, Minnesota
Scott and Mira Perrizo, Lyons, Colorado
John A Schroeder, El Cajon, California
Melvin Sorensen, St Francis, Minnesota
Frank Wolfbauer, Anoka, Minnesota
Harold Wong, Bloomington, Minnesota

We would also like to thank Dave Gehrke, editor of "The Roller Journal" of Sleepy Eye, Minnesota for the information he contributed about Rollers for Chapter 2.

A big thank you to Scott Perrizo of Crossings Press, who did an excellent job of fine tuning the book.

We are grateful for the thorough work done by Charlie Foy, who wrote and published the first "Pigeons for Pleasure and Profit" in 1962. Most of the writing is still his.

But the pigeon fancy has evolved and grown, and we've attempted to address this in the sixth edition. The ceremonial release of white pigeons is a new cottage industry, and one of the many changes we have covered in this book.

We hope this book serves as a good starting point, and that it offers you some helpful assistance and encouragement as you experience the joys of raising pigeons.

INDEX